Victorian & Edwardian Fashion
A Photographic Survey

by
Alison Gernsheim

Dover Publications, Inc.
New York

This Dover edition, first published in 1963, is an unabridged and slightly
corrected republication of the work originally published by Faber and
Faber, London, in 1963 under the title *Fashion and Reality (1840–1914)*.

International Standard Book Number: 0-486-24205-6
Library of Congress Catalog Card Number: 81-67863

Manufactured in the United States of America
Dover Publications, Inc., 31 East 2nd Street, Mineola, N.Y. 11501

CONTENTS

PICTURE CREDIT

For the Dover edition, prints of the following 82 photographs were made available for direct reproduction by the
Gernsheim Collection, Humanities Research Center,
The University of Texas at Austin:
Nos. 4, 7, 16, 17, 30, 31, 37, 38, 43, 50, 54, 56, 57, 58, 62, 65, 66, 69, 70, 71, 77, 78, 81, 84, 88, 89, 90, 91, 94, 95, 96, 97, 98, 99, 100, 103, 105, 111, 112, 115, 118, 119, 124, 127, 128, 129, 130, 131, 132, 135, 141, 142, 143, 144, 147, 148, 150, 157, 158, 163, 165, 167, 168, 171, 172, 173, 174, 178, 180, 181, 182, 183, 184, 191, 196, 201, 202, 210, 217, 218, 233, 234.

NOTES ON THE PHOTOGRAPHS

Sources: All the illustrations are from original photographs in the Gernsheim Collection except the following:

Mrs. Arthur Barrett, 204; Bibliothéque Nationale, Paris, 55; Hector Bolitho, 80; Central Press Photos, 226; Anthony Denny, 16; George Eastman House, Rochester, 136; Staatliche Landesbildstelle Hamburg, 11; Dr. H. Nickel, Halle, 6; Paul Popper Ltd., 112; Radio Times/ Hulton Picture Library, 63, 193, 213, 214, 216, 220, 222, 224–5; Royal Library, Windsor Castle, 30, 31, 35, 50, 57, 172, 234; Scottish National Portrait Gallery, 1, 2; Prof. Rudolf Skopec, Prague, 7; Harold White, 5.

(Between pages 32 and 33)

1   Mrs. Napier. Calotype by David Octavius Hill and Robert Adamson, Edinburgh, *c.* 1845. Striped silk dress with pointed bodice. Mrs. Napier wore a lace cap under her bonnet of coal scuttle form with internal trimming.

2   The Grierson sisters. Calotype by D. O. Hill and R. Adamson, Edinburgh, *c.* 1845. The little girls have long ringlets and tartan dresses.

3   Miss Dorothy Draper. Daguerreotype by Prof. John W. Draper, New York, summer 1840. One of the earliest successful portraits. Drawn bonnet with internal wreath of flowers; the brim opening is not oval as in most bonnets of this date, but circular. Muslin pelerine, Victoria sleeve.

4   Queen Victoria's going-away bonnet after her marriage on 10 February 1840. Now in the London Museum. Trimmed with white roses and orange blossom, lace veil, *bavolet* shading the neck. Daguerreotype.

5   W. H. Fox Talbot, inventor of the Calotype process of photography. Daguerreotype by Antoine Claudet, F.R.S. London, 1844. 'Parricide' collar and very tall top hat.

6   A lady. Daguerreotype by A. Schwendler, Dresden, *c.* 1844. Striped silk dress, bodice *en pelerine*, cap with bunches of white berries in front of ears.

7   Lady in checked dress with one wide flounce on skirt, two flounces on upper part of sleeve; poke bonnet and veil. Gentleman in dark frock coat (unfastened), light trousers and light top hat. Daguerreotype. Prague, *c.* 1842.

8   Fräulein Reimer, Frau Stelzner, Fräulein Mathilde von Braunschweig. Daguerreotype by C. F. Stelzner, Hamburg, *c.* 1842. Frau Stelzner, though married and not young, wears no cap. Her hair style and Frl. Reimer's show the basket-plait at the back and rather short side curls. Frl. von Braunschweig's hair is arranged smoothly over the ears; her afternoon dress of patterned material has a low-cut bertha.

9   David Octavius Hill and the Misses Morris. Calotype by Robert Adamson, Edinburgh, 1843–45. The plain tight sleeves and low necks of the sisters are typical of the first half of the 'forties. The artist and photographer D. O. Hill wears a light country suit of the type that developed into the lounge suit, and a tartan waistcoat.

10 Lady Mary Ruthven. Calotype by D. O. Hill and R. Adamson, Edinburgh, *c.* 1845. Striped silk dress, black lace shawl and poke bonnet with bavolet and veil.

Notes on the Photographs

11 An outing of the Hamburg Artists' Club, May 1843. Daguerreotype by C. F. Stelzner. Frock coats, figured waistcoats and top hats. Nearly all wear the new turned-out fairly low collar.

12 Miss McCandlish. Calotype by D. O. Hill and R. Adamson, Edinburgh, c. 1843. Low-necked dress and wide-brimmed straw garden hat.

13 Miss Chalmers and her brother. Calotype by D. O. Hill and R. Adamson, Edinburgh, c. 1843. Miss Chalmer's dress is of fancy striped silk; her brother appears to be wearing a day dress coat with cut-in. The combination of guitar and cornet must have produced some rather strange music.

14 A lady. Daguerreotype. Milan, c. 1845. The bold stripes of the material are used to accentuate the point of the bodice, with low neck-line dipping in front à la grecque.

15 A gentleman. Daguerreotype attributed to Richard Beard, London, c. 1845. Light waistcoat with revers, spotted necktie, the new form of collar. Hair curled forward over the ears, and side-whiskers.

16 A lady with reading-glass. Daguerreotype by A. Claudet, London, c. 1843. Dress of silk with small tartan pattern, tight sleeves trimmed with passementerie, high chemisette. Finely braided loops of hair leaving the ears exposed.

17 A gentleman. Daguerreotype, c. 1845. Light checked country jacket and waistcoat, scarf neckcloth almost hiding shirt, and hair curled forward in front of the ears. He is holding 'Bell's Life & Sport'.

18 A gentleman. Daguerreotype by E. Kilburn, London, c. 1850. His stand-up collar and broad tie are rather old-fashioned, but the oval opening of the waistcoat is probably not earlier than 1850. Side-whiskers.

19 A lady. Daguerreotype by J. E. Mayall, London, c. 1849. This and No. 24 show the smaller bonnet of the late 'forties with round-sectioned brim.

20 Gioachino Rossini. Daguerreotype. Paris, c. 1852. Dark frock coat, light waistcoat, top hat.

21 A lady. Daguerreotype by William Telfer, London, c. 1848. Striped silk dress, much jewellery, and wreath of flowers in hair arranged with short curls high on the temples in the style of the early 1830s.

22 A gentleman. Daguerreotype by Howie, Edinburgh, c. 1845. Whiskers, moustache, and a fringe under the chin which is clean-shaven. Fancy necktie in barrel knot.

23 Baroness de Späth. Daguerreotype by A. Claudet, London, 1852. Strongly striped silk dress with pelerine trimming, cap coming well forward over the ears as in the 'forties.

24 A lady. Daguerreotype by William Telfer, London, c. 1849. The round-sectioned bonnet has interior trimming of cherries and lace, exterior trimming and fastening of broad ribbon with a pattern of purple pansies (the original is hand-coloured). Sleeves widen to show embroidered white engageantes.

25 A lady. Daguerreotype by A. Claudet, London, c. 1851. Evening dress of patterned silk with many flounces; black lace scarf edged with quilled ribbon; wreath in hair which is dressed in the style of the 'forties.

26 Young girl in riding habit, gauntlet gloves and wide-brimmed Amazon hat. c. 1855.

27 Eleanor Cooper and baby, by George Cooper. 1856. Paisley shawl and small bonnet very far back on head; the baby's bonnet is ruffled round the edge.

28 At the ball, c. 1853–4. The double or flounced skirts are not yet very wide and there is no sign of hoops. Wreaths worn at the back of the head.

29 The Geography Lesson. Stereoscopic daguerreotype by A. Claudet, London, 1851. The

little girls' ringlets and 'spaniel' loops of hair and their frocks closely follow adult fashions. The little boy on the right wears a frock like a girl's.

30 Queen Victoria in Court dress after a Drawing-room at Buckingham Palace on 11 March 1854. By Roger Fenton. Her elaborate dress has apparently no artificial stiffening. The skirt is caught up in many places by small bouquets, and the brocade train falls from the waist.

31 Prince Albert, by J. E. Mayall, Osborne, August 1855. Dark morning coat, checked waistcoat with big revers, fancy trousers, and light-coloured wide-awake hat.

32 Sir Rowland Hill, by Maull & Polyblank, London, c. 1858. Frock coat (which looks like keeping on an overcoat indoors), light trousers and waistcoat of different materials. Old-fashioned 'parricide' collar.

33 David Octavius Hill and his sister Mary Watson, Edinburgh, c. 1858. Frock coat, checked waistcoat and wide-awake hat. Mrs. Watson's extremely wide sleeves are right up-to-date but her cap is old-fashioned.

34 The Misses Lutwidge playing chess, by Lewis Carroll, c. 1857. Tartan silk dress trimmed with fringe, and dress trimmed with *passementerie*. Both bodices are in the form with *bretelles*, and the collars and *engageantes* are of *broderie anglaise*.

35 Prince Alfred, the tutor F. W. Gibbs, and the Prince of Wales. By Roger Fenton, Windsor, 8 February 1854. The young princes wear short jackets, light waistcoats and checked trousers, military style peaked caps. Mr. Gibbs has early taken to the new morning coat, under which he wears a wide-lapelled tartan waistcoat. Tie in barrel knot.

36 A little girl. Daguerreotype by Anson, New York, 1855. The stiff bertha looks far too large for the child. Petticoat edged with *broderie anglaise*, button boots.

37 George Wilson, by George Washington Wilson, Aberdeen, 1857. The two-year-old boy wears a home-made frock of checked material.

38 The Misses Dingwall-Fordyce of Brucklay Castle, by G. W. Wilson, Aberdeen, c. 1858. The little girls' capes are edged with fringe. Large straw hats trimmed with an ostrich feather, pantalettes bordered with *broderie anglaise*, and boots.

39 Mrs Fisher, by G. W. Wilson, Aberdeen, c. 1857. Double skirt with broad striped border and scalloped edge; basqued bodice trimmed with fringe, closed undersleeves in Bishop form.

40 Sir Archibald Alison, by Maull & Polyblank, London, c. 1858. In the late 'fifties tartan patterns were particularly fashionable, but the Scottish historian seems to have rather overdone it in choosing different tartans for his trousers and waistcoat.

41 Young lady by Maull & Polyblank, London, c. 1857. Basqued bodice with wide sleeves, double skirt with striped border, and large straw hat. She has old-fashioned ringlets and wears no crinoline.

42 An unusually lively portrait for 1856. The waistcoat and trousers with a diagonal pattern are of the same material, with a dark morning coat and checked necktie.

43 Mother and daughter, 1858. Double skirted dress trimmed with black velvet chevrons; and dress with the 'Bayadère' stripes featured for several years in the mid-'fifties. Frilled sunshade lined with white.

44 Princesses Helena and Louise, by Roger Fenton, c. 1857. Tartan dresses worn over a crinoline, black jackets with a basque, feathered hats.

45 A group photographed at Osborne by Colonel D. F. de Ros, March 1858. L to R. Hon. Emily Cathcart, Lord Colville, Lady Churchill, Colonel Biddulph. Miss Cathcart is informally dressed, her drawn-up skirt revealing a white petticoat, and hat of the kind

worn in the country. Lady Churchill is more formal; so are the frock coats and top hats of the gentlemen. Lord Colville wears a mourning band round his hat, but checked trousers.

46 Mrs. William Blake, *c.* 1854. Double skirt with scalloped edge, elaborate sleeves, *broderie anglaise* on *engageantes* and collar, hair bracelet.

47 Michael Faraday, by Maull & Polyblank, London, *c.* 1855. For lecturing in the day-time Faraday wears 'half dress' — a cut-in tail coat, which was soon relegated to evening dress. Watered silk waistcoat, light trousers.

48 Alfred Tennyson, by James Mudd, *c.* 1857. The poet wears a wide-awake hat and country jacket, which in this year had fullness at the shoulders.

49 Gentleman with tall top hat, morning coat and matching waistcoat, small-checked trousers with prominent side seams; his long side-whiskers are almost Dundrearies. *c.* 1858.

50 The Princess Royal (later the Empress Frederick of Germany) in her confirmation dress. Windsor, 20 March 1856, by W. Bambridge. The white silk dress has a skirt composed of five vandyked flounces.

51 The Duet, *c.* 1857. The pianists wear evening dresses of some light colour with black lace flounces and bertha, and flowers at the back of the head.

52 Drawn-up skirts, round seaside hats, morning coats and top hats on Margate beach, *c.* 1858.

53 Sitting on the sill of a French window at Ockham Park, Miss Carr is equipped for reading with an Ugly to shield her eyes, a shawl against draughts, and kid gloves. Drawn-up skirt, but clearly no crinoline. *c.* 1860.

54 Lord Brougham, by Maull & Polyblank, London, 1856. Old-fashioned 'parricide' collar and broad necktie, frock coat and checked trousers with wide black braid down the side seams.

55 A crinoline shop in Paris, *c.* 1862. Crinolines were sold by Th. But along with lace and underclothes.

56 Princess Marie of Hohenzollern-Sigmaringen, 1858. Skirt with three flounces edged with a narrow band of velvet, basqued bodice, plush hat. Pantalettes and ankle length boots.

57 Princess Frederick William of Prussia (the Princess Royal) in the dress she wore at a ball at Buckingham Palace on 1 June 1859. Very large crinoline, two wide lace flounces on the skirt and narrow ones forming short sleeves.

58 The Empress Eugénie, by Disdéri, Paris, 1859. Outdoor dress and jacket trimmed with broad bands of stiff pleating; plain *engageantes* ending in a cuff. Bonnet edged with flowers, and very wide strings.

59 Queen Victoria and the Prince Consort, by J. E. Mayall, 1861. The Queen's dress is of flounced check material worn over a crinoline, with a transparent black shawl. The Prince's coat, which looks like a frock coat, is probably a very slightly cut away morning coat. Striped waistcoat with wide revers.

60 Lady in dress of vertically striped material, the skirt trimmed with two broad bands of a darker colour. Round and slightly high waist with narrow belt, and a new type of sleeve. *c.* 1862.

(Between pages 48 and 49)

61 The Duchess of Manchester ('the Double Duchess', later Duchess of Devonshire) by Camille Silvy, London, *c.* 1863. Ball dress with numerous narrow flounces on skirt and wide asymmetrically placed flounce of white lace. Large wreath of flowers in hair.

62 Princess Mary of Cambridge (later Duchess of Teck), by Camille Silvy, London, *c.* 1861.

Ten narrow scalloped flounces in two groups on skirt; bodice with point at waist, which went out of fashion for day dresses the following year. Round hat with feather.

63   Group at a country house, by H. W. Verschoyle, *c*. 1862. The lady in a striped dress is almost eclipsed by her crinoline when sitting down. The man is wearing a light-coloured lounge suit; the lady with croquet mallet has a drawn-up skirt and striped petticoat.

64   Group on the terrace of a country house, *c*. 1863, by Charles Nègre. Lord Brougham with family and friends at Cannes. There are two 'short' dresses, a Tweedside with light bowler hat, a lounge suit (with shorter jacket than the Tweedside), and in the middle an old gentleman with 'parricide' collar and wide-awake hat.

65   The Prince and Princess of Wales at Sandringham, autumn 1863. By the London Stereoscopic Company. The Princess wears a plain jacket and dress, with which a hat, not a bonnet, was correct. The Prince's 'lounging suit of "dittoes" ' looks rather modern, except that it fastens on the top button only. He was one of the first to wear a round-crowned hard felt hat — i.e. a bowler.

66   The Prince of Wales, by J. E. Mayall, March 1863. Braid-edged frock coat and waistcoat to match, checked trousers and cravat.

67   Mrs. James Bache, *c*. 1863. *Tablier* of narrow scalloped flounces on skirt and three at the bottom. A loose cape with wide black lace border hides the waist and produces a pyramid form, terminating in the 'spoon' bonnet.

68   The Duchess of Sutherland, by Disdéri, Paris. *c*. 1864. Winter mantle of dark velvet heavily braided and frogged in military style; astrakhan collar and cap. The flounces beneath look rather incongruous.

69   Two evening dresses *c*. 1864 trimmed with bold meanders applied in black ribbon. Hair flat on top with a roll each side.

70   The crinoline is fairly straight in front, extending much further behind. Basqued velvet jacket with the new masculine coat-sleeve, trimmed with bobble-fringe and braid. Similar hair style to No. 69 with the addition of long ringlets. *c*. 1864.

71   Princess Alice of Hesse and one of her daughters, photographed at Balmoral by G. W. Wilson, *c*. 1866. Walking dress with skirt drawn up over a striped petticoat. The edge of the dress is trimmed with broad pleating divided at intervals by dark-coloured tabs; the matching jacket is bound with braid.

72   Winter walking dress, *c* 1863. An early 'At Home' photograph by William Cox, Northampton. Skirt drawn up showing 'short' petticoat trimmed with dark horizontal bands. Short sealskin jacket and small barrel muff. A hat is worn as the dress is informal.

73   Lady Diana Beauclerk, by F. R. Window. London, *c*. 1866. Evening dress with panniered overskirt back and front, square neckline and ruffles on sleeves.

74   The Princess of Solmes, Comtesse Ratazzi, in evening dress, by Disdéri, Paris, *c*. 1867. Velvet bodice and long tunic bordered with lace, opening asymmetrically over a skirt with narrow tulle flounces arranged diagonally in groups separated by bands of trimming. Empire style diadem and long ringlets at the back.

75   Jane Morris posed by D. G. Rossetti, July 1865. (Photographer unknown). The Pre-Raphaelites disapproved of crinolines.

76   Dr. Mary Walker, *c*. 1865. In this sensible kind of costume with tunic and trousers Dr. Walker served with the Federal Army during the American Civil War, and was taken prisoner by the Confederates. The prejudice of women clerks in the U.S. Treasury Department against her persistence in wearing rational dress prevented Dr. Walker taking up her position there.

11

77 Country suit consisting of lounge jacket, knickerbockers and waistcoat of matching checked material. *c.* 1867.

78 Lady's riding-habit, mid-'sixties. A top hat was often worn, instead of the round hat in this photograph by R. Cade, Ipswich.

79 Woman alpinist in crinoline on the Grindelwald glacier, by Adolphe Braun, *c.* 1863.

80 Croquet players in 'short' crinolines, *c.* 1866. The fashion for two contrasting colours is shown on the right, where the narrow sleeves, headed with a braid 'jockey' well below the shoulder, match the petticoat. The dark upper skirt is scalloped at the edge. The man wears a lounge suit and square-crowned hard hat.

81 A girl, by Ghémar frères, Brussels, *c.* 1862. The flounced dress, wide frilled sleeves and feathered hat look absurdly adult, in contrast with the more sensible garb of the English girl in No. 82.

82 Ella Monier Williams, by Lewis Carroll, 1866. Pleated easy-fitting bodice with loose sleeves, small crinoline, and 'Alice in Wonderland' hair.

83 Lady with stereoscope, by J. Horsburgh, *c.* 1867. Dress with peplum trimmed with bands of black velvet. Narrow crinoline.

84 The Princess of Wales, by Disdéri, *c.* 1866. Dress of watered-silk with the new straighter outline. The heavy lace is applied round the lower part of the skirt, and to simulate a tunic.

85 A group in the country, *c.* 1867. The dresses all have a high round waist and straight-sided skirt over a fairly small crinoline. The third from the left has a short *casaque* to match. Top hats had become much lower the preceding year.

86 Archery group, *c.* 1868. Several of the younger women have drawn up skirts and two have a pannier effect at the back. Small hats perched in front of the chignon. The men wear lounge jackets not matching the trousers, and bowler hats.

87 A family at Wimbledon, *c.* 1869. 'Empire' style dresses without crinolines (except possibly on extreme right). The standing woman has a Marie Antoinette fichu; the old lady has old-fashioned curls and her husband a light top hat.

88 The Empress Elisabeth of Austria, by Rabending, Vienna, *c.* 1869. Trained 'Empire' dress of velvet.

89 Lady in trained velvet 'Empire' dress, by Jabez Hughes, Ryde, I.o.W. *c.* 1869.

90 Mary Helen Ferguson, by I. Wood, Aberdeen, *c.* 1868. Elaborate applications of dark braid and other trimming in vandykes. Very narrow crinoline, hard round straw hat.

91 Simple house dress without a crinoline; the wide sash gives a very slight bustle effect. by F. Gutekunst, Philadelphia. *c.* 1870.

92 The alternative to the 'Empire' dress in No. 89: the Hon. Mrs. George Pennant (later Baroness Penrhyn) in a walking dress of checked material worn over a narrow crinoline, *c.* 1868. The tunic is caught up at the sides.

93 A lady, by Maull & Co., London, *c.* 1869. The smooth round chignon on top of the head was one of the styles of this year (see also No. 89). The short tunic, caught up at the sides, shows signs of a small bustle.

94 A *casquette*, *c.* 1869, by Elliott & Fry, London.

95 A 'lamballe plateau' *c.* 1869, by Icilio Calzolari, Milan.

96 Elaborate hair style of 1868–9, by the London Stereoscopic Co.

97 Lady Bute, by James Russell & Sons, Chichester, *c.* 1871. Small hat trimmed with lilac and other flowers.

98 Outdoor dress and matching jacket trimmed with broad light bands. Double skirt of

short tunic and underskirt both edged with pleated flounce. The bustle is hardly noticeable. *c.* 1870

99   A lady, by C. S. Cork, Hadleigh, *c.* 1870. Cloth day dress trimmed with three rows of black velvet, the cuffs and upper skirt or tunic edged with pleated flounces. Bustle. Chatelaine hanging from brooch.

100   The Comtesse de Pourtalès, by Le Jeune, Paris, 1870. Hair style and aigret the same as No. 113, but as the photographer was appointed to the Prince Imperial the portrait must have been taken in 1870. Reception dress with velvet bodice and train over a light skirt composed of alternate rows of *bouillons* and flounces increasing in width downwards.

101   Prince Leopold and Princess Louise, 1870. Like his brother the Prince of Wales, Prince Leopold was quick to take up new fashions, and wears a forerunner of the Homburg hat and a new kind of knotted tie. Reefer jacket. His sister has a fur-trimmed short jacket and striped dress with a tunic of different material.

102   A lady, by G. W. Wilson, Aberdeen, *c.* 1874. Enormous high plaited chignon, striped dress with bustle, fluted full at neck.

103   A lady, by G. W. Wilson, Aberdeen, *c.* 1872. Enormous plaited chignon, dark silk dress with bustle.

104   A lady with parrot, by Liébert, Paris, *c.* 1875. Trained bustle dress of tartan silk of complicated construction; long curls.

105   The Hon. L. Kerr, *c.* 1873, did not wear the exaggerated style of Nos. 102–104. The bustle of her velvet dress is very moderate, and so is her chignon.

106   Mrs. T. R. T. Hodgson, *c.* 1872. The old lady clings to her old-fashioned shawl, bonnet, and curls on the temples.

107   A lady, *c.* 1873. Bustle dress trimmed with fringe like the chair, and with a train like the peacock in the decorative border. Elaborately trimmed small cap.

108   Mrs. Rousby in yachting dress and 'boater'. *c.* 1870.

109   Viscountess Newport, by W. & D. Downey, London, *c.* 1878. Striped cuirasse bodice with light sleeves, darker skirt. Small hat worn at the back of the head, trimmed with currants.

110   A lady, by R. F. Barnes, *c.* 1876. Long velvet Princess polonaise (tunic and bodice in one) edged with fringe and with an ornamental pocket at the back. The underskirt extending into a train has several rows of narrow flounces.

111   The Princess of Wales (right) and her sister Dagmar, later the Czarina, during the latter's visit to London in 1873. Identical bustle dresses of plain and spotted material, with train. The underskirt has a wide border of pleats and flounces.

112   The Prince of Wales, *c.* 1875. Morning coat, light trousers with pronounced side seam (not a crease), top hat.

113   The Princess of Wales, by Horatio Nelson King, London, *c.* 1874. Evening or dinner dress reminiscent of the eighteenth century with its lace ruffles, jewelled buttons and bow. The velvet of the bodice combines with the light-coloured stiff silk of the skirt in a complicated train.

114   The young sportsmen's lounge jackets are of a special type called University coats, cut away at a very sharp angle. Breeches and knickerbockers to match, respectively, and square crowned hard felt hats. Early 'seventies.

115   The Prince of Wales, by W. & D. Downey, October 1876, when he brought down one of the herd of wild bulls in the park at Chillingham Castle. Lounge jacket, knickerbockers, waistcoat, shirt and gaiters are all checked. Deerstalker cap.

116 Tennis in tied-back skirts and trains, *c.* 1878.

117 Tricycling costume consisting of patrol jacket, close-fitting breeches, boots and small cap. The 'penny farthing' is a Humber Roadster with 58″ diameter wheel, 1878–79. By Benda, Prague.

118 Resting after tennis, *c.* 1875. One of the earliest tennis pictures, since lawn tennis was patented in 1874. The bustle, sleeves and neck ruffle of the woman on the right would seem to bear this out. However, the two younger women are wearing the fashions of 1875. The male player wears light-coloured knickerbockers, very thick socks, ankle boots, and a bowler.

119 Daughters of the Duke of Buckingham, Governor General of Madras, *c.* 1877. Their riding habits have a tight bodice with postilion basque and narrow sleeves. The skirts are very long, and the top hats tilted forward.

(*Between pages 64 and 65*)

120 A lady, by Theodor Prümm, Berlin, 1878–9. A summer dress in which the daintiness of the material counteracts the otherwise heavy effect of the complicated structure. Tied-back skirt and train.

121 A lady, by Hills & Saunders, Oxford, *c.* 1877. Cuirasse bodice, underskirt and train of different material from the light-coloured plastron and diagonally arranged overskirt. Gainsborough hat.

122 Miss Ada Dyas, by Horatio Nelson King, London, *c.* 1875. Dark plastron on bodice giving a waistcoat effect, narrow sleeves with elaborate cuff. Front of skirt trimmed with three horizontal pleated flounces headed with bands of material; the overskirt at the back trimmed with a row of buttons.

123 A lady, by Fratelli Vianelli, Venice, *c.* 1878. Pointed cuirasse bodice of different material from the tight sleeves and the skirt, which is almost hidden by flounces and fringe. No bustle (it is a studio rock projecting), and train. Small velvet hat.

124 Ball dress trimmed with many narrow flounces and sprays of artificial flowers, pleated train, *c.* 1877–78.

125 Ball dress of satin-striped silk. By F. Gutekunst, Philadelphia, *c.* 1877.

126 A lady, *c.* 1879. Cuirasse bodice and horizontally draped long tunic of one material; gauged plastron, sleeves, gauged trimming down sides of skirt and underskirt of another shade.

127 A lady, by E. T. Church, Belfast, *c.* 1879. Dark velvet long cuirasse bodice with light sleeves; light skirt trimmed with the velvet.

128 Winston Churchill and his aunt. Dublin, 1880. Plain high-fastening lounge jacket and breeches. Although not wearing a sailor suit he has a sailor's cap with the name 'Invincible'. Lady Leslie's velvet jacket has satin revers matching her horizontally draped skirt.

129 The Countess of Dudley and her daughter, by W. & D. Downey, London, *c.* 1880. Very long cuirasse bodice and skirt with horizontal pleating; small bonnet worn far back. The child's dark stockings and button boots look rather heavy compared with her frilly light dress (see also No. 135). Feathered hat.

130 Oscar Wilde in the eighteenth-century style suit which he wore when lecturing in America in 1882.

131 Lady in Court dress, by Window & Grove, London, *c.* 1880. Tube-shaped white satin dress with horizontal pleating at sides and bead embroidery. Separate long brocade

train. White feathers in fan and hair. These are not upstanding as they should be for presentation, and Queen Victoria at this period objected to the small feathers worn by some ladies.

132 Marriage of a daughter of the Duke of Buckingham (on right) at Stowe House, c 1883. In the 'eighties a morning coat was worn at weddings, the frock coat being temporarily out of favour. The bridesmaids' white or light-coloured dresses have draped apron fronts and a side panel of dark material; their bustles are not very large.

133 Three men and a boat, picnicking by the Thames, by William Taunt, c. 1883. Casual clothes, though more of them than today; cricket caps and 'boater'.

134 Scarborough, by G. W. Wilson, c. 1884. The little girl has a feminine version of the sailor suit. The men in lounge jackets wear white flannel trousers, bowler and 'boater' respectively.

135 Queen Louise of Denmark and her granddaughters the Princesses Louise, Victoria and Maud of Wales. Athens, August 1882. The Queen's flowered silk dress has two flounces on the skirt. The young princesses have draped and flounced skirts which contrast with the plain bodices, 'boaters', thick stockings and button boots.

136 Miss Coleman jumping, by Eadweard Muybridge, Philadelphia, 21 September 1885. Taken for a study of animal locomotion.

137 Mrs. Finney, by Lord Walter Campbell, c. 1884. Tailor-made suit with kilted skirt and scarf drapery at hips.

138 Mrs. Langtry, by Lafayette, London, c. 1888. Reception dress with train from the waist, over a brocade skirt with a strong pattern. The complete absence of sleeves was an innovation which did not find general acceptance.

139 Four women at Portelet Bay, Jersey, c. 1889. Little or no bustle, skirts hanging straight, slightly humped shoulders to the sleeve.

140 Paddling at Skipness, c. 1883. The central figure has a slightly panniered skirt and back drapery over a small bustle.

141 The women members of this American tennis club have devised a fairly practical costume, but the men have made no attempt in this direction and play in lounge suits and bowlers. c. 1887.

142 Tricycling, c. 1884. The woman has a similar tailor-made to No. 137 except that the bodice opens in front like a jacket. Her companion wears a patrol jacket and tight breeches.

143 Miss Burnett, by G. W. Wilson, Aberdeen, c. 1884. Lace flounces and stuffed birds were particularly fashionable this year.

144 Three sisters in similar dresses — perhaps bridesmaids — and their brother in a sailor suit, by G. W. Wilson, Aberdeen, c. 1884. Scarf drapery at hips, cascades of lace on skirt.

145 Princess Beatrice and Prince Henry of Battenberg, by Elliott & Fry, London. February 1885. The Princess's plain bodice fastens down the front with innumerable buttons and extends over the bustle. Pleated 'apron' over the kilted skirt. Her fiancé wears a morning coat and winged collar.

146 Lady Brooke (later Countess of Warwick) by Herbert Barraud, London, c. 1886. Fur-edged embroidered *visite* over a white evening dress. The full extent of the bustle at its mightiest can be appreciated in this picture, No. 150, 153 and 161. Lady Brooke's curled fringe is perhaps false.

147 Venus, c. 1887. Dress of boldly striped material, skirt slightly gathered up. Hair in a knot on top.

Notes on the Photographs

148 Miss Young, *c.* 1884. Fur-edged bodice, scarf drapery, small bustle.

149 A lady, by G. W. Wilson, Aberdeen, *c.* 1889. Striped silk dress with bands of jet embroidery; no drapery, and probably little or no bustle.

150 Miss Leila Johnston. White ball dress trimmed with ribbon, net or tulle train falling over an enormous bustle. The effect is rather spoilt by a knitted shawl.

151 The purpose of these military-looking costumes photographed by G. W. Wilson of
152 Aberdeen is unknown to me. The one with scarf drapery is a year or two earlier than the still more severe uniforms in No. 152 : probably 1885 and 1888–9 respectively.

153 Hamburg harbour, by Srna, Vienna, *c.* 1886. Apron-fronted skirt over striped under-skirt; large bustle. Two of the women, though German, wear Tam O'Shanters; the third, a feathered hat.

154 Horace Hutchinson in golf suit, by Walery, London, 1889. Checked jacket and knicker-bockers, long stockings and spats, rather thin shoes, small cap.

155 Skating in Vienna, by Oscar Van Zel, *c.* 1887. The stiff attitude of the people in 'frozen motion' is characteristic of the bustle period. Several of the women wear 'flower-pot' hats.

156 A party of tourists crossing the Mer de Glace near Chamonix — the women in bustles and carrying sunshades, *c.* 1885.

157 Princess Louise, Duchess of Fife, at her Scottish home Mar Lodge, by W. & D. Downey. September 1889. Plain tailor-made with very high collar, small bustle, and 'flower-pot' hat.

158 Princess Victoria of Wales at Frogmore, photographed by the Princess of Wales, 1889. Plain dark jacket, striped skirt without a bustle, sailor hat and — like her sister in No. 157 — an umbrella.

159 Tea in a garden by the Thames near Cliveden, *c.* 1888–9. Lounge suits, 'boaters', summer dresses, and on the right a tailor-made.

160 Mr. and Mrs. Gladstone with Lord Rendel and his daughters at Naples, January 1889. Mr. Gladstone's light-coloured bowler has a beehive crown. Mrs. Gladstone, being elderly, wears a cap. Her long sealskin coat is bordered with sable.

161 Miss Julia Neilson, by Walery, London, *c.* 1887. Her satin ball dress is complicated in cut, with a cross-over bodice; large bustle. Hair in a knot on top of the head came into fashion in 1887.

162 Domestic interior, by Robert Slingsby, Norwich, 1889. The mother is in evening dress, father in a morning suit, the daughters in plain morning frocks. The pampas grass, Japanese screen and fan in the fireplace are characteristic.

163 George Bernard Shaw, by Frederick Hollyer, London, *c.* 1890. Wearing one of his Jaeger suits.

164 Oscar Wilde, by W. & D. Downey, London, 1890. The frock coat had just returned to favour. Wilde's is double-breasted with silk-faced lapels, and appears to be dark grey, not black. Broad knotted tie, striped trousers.

165 Agnes Bright, Ethel Spiller and Edith Robinson setting out on a walking tour *c.* 1890. Although the photograph was taken at Leamington Spa, by Graham, the climbing pole grasped by Edith and the umbrella of Ethel incline me to believe that the goal of these emancipated women was the Lake District.

166 Lord and Lady Rendel, their daughters, son-in-law Mr. Goodhart and grandchild. September 1890. Lord Rendel wears a lounge suit and square hard hat, Mr. Goodhart a small cap. Miss Rendel is sportily dressed compared with Mrs. Goodhart and her hat

has a wider brim than had been worn for a long time. Sleeves have not yet begun to expand.

167   The Duchess of Albany with her children, nieces and nephews. Claremont, April 1890. The youngest princes wear a sailor suit and Scottish dress; the baby on the rocking-horse is over-burdened with clothes and a big hat.

168   Woman with little boy in Scottish dress on a donkey, c. 1893. 'Crumpled' big sleeves, broad-brimmed flat straw hat worn rather high and straight on the head.

169   Aubrey Beardsley, by Frederick Holyer, c. 1894. After this date, his morning coat would have four buttons, not three. Plain dark waistcoat, striped trousers, butterfly bow tie. Centre-parted hair combed forward — a new style.

170   Mrs. Saxton Noble tricycling c. 1893. Tailor-made suit with three-quarter length jacket, full sleeves; flat straw hat with brim wider than a 'boater'.

171   The Kaiserin Augusta Victoria, consort of Kaiser Wilhelm II, 1891. Evening or dinner dress with draped bodice, shoulder knots and full sleeves. Diamond star in hair.

172   The Duchess Maximilian of Bavaria, by Dittmar, Munich, 1892 (with inscription to Queen Victoria, 1893). Trained black dress with lace sleeves, Medici collar; diamond crescent in hair.

173   Princess Marie of Edinburgh and her fiancé Prince Ferdinand of Rumania. June 1892. Light-coloured dress with full sleeves above ending in dark velvet below the elbow. Similar velvet forms a vest front with high collar.

174   Lady Randolph Churchill, by W. & D. Downey, London, 1893. Dark satin evening dress trimmed with lighter velvet sash and rosettes. Revers of lace extending over large sleeves; aigrette in hair.

175   Girls in cycling bloomers on the quay at Boulogne, 1897. By Paul Martin. Print by courtesy of Leonard Russell.

176   Coney Island, N.Y. c. 1899. Women have rather long-skirt bathing costumes and some of them wear stockings. Men's swim suits are often striped.

(Between pages 80 and 81)

177   Mrs. Weir, by F. Hoeffler, Davos, c. 1899. Tailor-made suit with three-quarter length jacket, waistcoat, high starched collar and cuffs.

178   The Archduchess Stephanie, widow of Rudolph von Habsburg, by Alice Hughes. London, c. 1895. Tailor-made suit with big sleeves, manly collar and tie. Straw hat on the lines of a 'boater'.

179   The Ladies Alexandra and Maud Duff (daughters of Princess Louise, Duchess of Fife) by Alice Hughes. London, 1895. Frilly white hats and coats with full sleeves.

180   The Princess of Wales at Mar Lodge, by W. & D. Downey, 1894. Coat and skirt of small checked material, short jacket with full sleeves, 'Fedora' hat.

181   The Infanta Eulalia of Spain, by Alice Hughes, London, c. 1897. Evening dress of lace over satin; the back part of the skirt is a train of brocade trimmed with dark fur. Neo-classical hair style and tiara.

182   The Duchess of Connaught, by Alice Hughes, London, 1895. Satin evening dress with large sleeves partly covered by a lace flounce.

183   The Princess of Wales, Princess Maud of Wales and her fiancé Prince Charles of Denmark (later King Haakon of Norway). The Princesses have balloon sleeves; the Prince is in morning coat and striped trousers. By W. & D. Downey, May 1896.

184   The Duchess of York (later Queen Mary) by Lafayette, Dublin, c. 1897.

Notes on the Photographs

185 (Sir) Austen Chamberlain, c. 1900. Light tweed lounge suit, very high collar, and knotted tie passing through a tie-ring.

186 Mr. and Mrs. Frederick MacMillan and friends, August 1901. The three visitors wear the popular bolero jacket and elaborate hats; Mrs. MacMillan being at home has no hat, though her husband wears a light or white Homburg.

187 Navy serge skirt, plain white blouse, 'boater' and sunshade were considered very practical for the seaside. The child's woollen bathing suit has rather long legs, high neck, and sleeves. August 1901.

188 Light coat and skirt with bands of trimming, white Oxford shoes, flat cap with spotted veil. The man wears a lounge jacket and matching knickerbockers, long thick socks and a small tweed cap, c. 1902.

189 In flat motoring cap, wrapped in a fur rug, the lady is going for a quiet drive with her uniformed white-gloved chauffeur. April 1902.

190 This woman motorist is prepared for a fast drive on dusty roads, wearing a dust-coat, thick veil to keep her hair clean, and goggles. c. 1905.

191 Women playing hockey, by W. & H. Manor, c. 1900. Blouses and long skirts, and hats that have to be clutched when running.

192 Queenie and Gertrude play billiards while waiting for the horseless carriage — or perhaps they only wear motoring caps for show. The high shoulders of Gertrude's short jacket are similar to the early 'nineties. c. 1903.

193 Visitors arriving at Henley station for the Regatta, c. 1904. Frilly summer dresses with pouched bodices, high necks; lingerie hats. 'Boaters' and white trousers for the men.

194 Balloon race at Ranelagh, July 1906. Elaborate gowns, flowered hats, sunshades and feather boas. Frock coats and top hats, with the exception of one man in lounge suit and 'boater'.

195 Miss Eleanor Souray by Bassano, London c. 1904. White dress with horizontal tucks above the hem; bodice and long basque of *broderie anglaise*. Wide-brimmed hat with white ostrich feathers.

196 Vera Blackhall, June 1905. Big white lingerie hat, long ringlets, white coat, gloves and sunshade, black stockings and button boots.

197 Miss Camille Clifford, the personification of the Gibson Girl, c. 1906.

198 The Archduchess Stephanie, by Alice Hughes, London, c. 1905. White dress with skirt similar to No. 195, jewelled dog-collar and hat with white ostrich feathers — a typical Casino toilet.

199 A lady, by H. Walter Barnett, London, c. 1906. A typical Edwardian dinner gown of filmy material, the skirt edged with several lace flounces, a narrower frill of lace at the neck, and loose transparent sleeves.

200 A lady, by Armand Daudoy. Namurs, c. 1903. White dress flaring at the hem, finely tucked bodice with slight pouch, long boa, and flat dark-coloured hat. Wide waistbelt with chatelaine and silver-chain purse; lorgnette.

201 Queen Alexandra with her daughters Princess Victoria (left) and Princess Louise, Duchess of Fife, in the magnificent dresses and jewels they wore at the wedding of Princess Margaret of Connaught to Prince Gustav of Sweden (now King Gustav VI) at Windsor Castle, 15 June 1905. The dresses, of some soft material, are embroidered all over with sequins. The diadem worn by Queen Alexandra is now displayed in the Queen's Gallery, Buckingham Palace.

202 A lady, c. 1906. Long-sleeved white dress with scarf hanging from a rosette high on the

bodice almost to the hem of the trained skirt. Hat trimmed above and below the tilted brim.

203 Group of Austrian Archdukes and Archduchesses, *c.* 1906. The ladies' dresses and hats seem too elaborate for the country scene. The man on the left in a Norfolk suit has creases down his knickerbockers.

204 Balloon race at Ranelagh, by Arthur Barrett, 1908. A less formal occasion than No. 194. One lady has a plain 'boater', the other a more dressy large hat covered with roses.

205 Miss Lily Elsie as 'The Merry Widow'. By Foulsham & Banfield, London, 1908. This was the first year of the heavy large-crowned hats and dresses on revived Empire lines. The cloak has a rather academic form.

206 Miss Marie George, by Bassano, London, *c.* 1911. Embroidered trained summer afternoon dress, striped jacket, sunshade with duck's head handle, and lavishly trimmed wide hat.

207 Colossal hat with ostrich plumes, sable stole and big muff, with a summer dress. *c.* 1910.

208 Mrs. Brown Potter, by Foulsham & Banfield, London, *c.* 1909. Black hat with transparent brim, the enormous crown made still larger with black feathers.

209 Mrs. Charles A. Wilson, Aberdeen, 1909. Plain tailor-made suit, high-necked blouse and 'boater'.

210 Miss Pauline Chase, by Reutlinger, Paris, *c.* 1910. A Paris tailor-made with trained skirt and long coat with chinchilla collar and cuffs. Wide hat with upstanding white feathers.

211 Sir George and Lady Alexander in Paris, *c.* 1910. Tunic dress, wide-brimmed hat with large flowers, and a white fox fur. Furs in the form of the complete animal only began to be worn in the present century.

212 Members of the Women's Freedom League of non-militant suffragists at a demonstration in Trafalgar Square, *c.* 1911. Simple white short dress, dark shoes and stockings with clocks; town tailor-made trimmed with braid. Emancipated women did not wear hobble skirts, but they succumbed to fashion as far as hats were concerned.

213 'Black Ascot', 1910. In mourning for Edward VII, all society women wore black. Tunics over hobble skirts, tassels, boas and hats large in crown and brim, trimmed with ostrich feathers. The man in a morning coat has black gloves and tie.

214 Lady Ormonde and Lady Constance Butler at Cowes, August 1910. Hobble skirts were out of the question for yachting. Plain navy blue coats and skirts of heavy cloth were worn, with 'boaters' or flat hats tied on with a thick veil as for motoring.

215 Marriage of the Archduke Karl — later the last Emperor of Austria-Hungary — to Princess Zita of Bourbon and Parma, 21 October 1911. The Emperor Franz Joseph is in the centre. The dresses are all too wide-skirted and sweeping to be fashionable, but were undoubtedly more graceful for a wedding than hobble skirts. The tiaras would have needed extensive alteration to bring them up to date, worn low on the forehead (see No. 219).

216 Yeomanry sports at Blenheim Palace, May 1911. The summer dresses, many of them white, all have rather high necks though no longer invariably extending right up the neck. Long gloves meet the sleeves. Wide, lavishly trimmed hats. The men are informally dressed in lounge suits.

217 Harem-skirted dresses and turbans designed by Paul Poiret to be worn at private parties. March 1911.

218 Trouser-skirt which caused a sensation at the Auteuil races, March 1911. If buttoned up at the side it would appear to be an ordinary hobble skirt.

219 Miss Vera Beringer, by Foulsham & Banfield, London, *c.* 1911. 'Empire' evening dress with short train, fox fur. Wide hair style with low filet and aigrette jutting out sideways. Very long-handled lorgnette.

220 A startling fashion at Auteuil races, July 1912. The short skirt, held up by the model still higher, was found very shocking. Wide flat hat with enormous hat-pin.

221 The new ballroom at the Hyde Park Hotel, by E. Walter Barnett, 1912. After being presented at Court, the debutantes laid aside their trains and feathers to dance. None has a hobble skirt, still less a harem skirt; all wear fairly simple 'Empire' dresses.

222 Ascot, 1913. These extraordinary dresses and hats with vertical plumes have something clown-like about them.

223 Miss Baden-Powell, Chief of the Girl Guides, *c.* 1913, by Mrs. Broom. Wrap-over hobble skirt, white fur stole, small hat with bird of paradise feathers extending backwards.

224 Fair in aid of Our Dumb Friends League, 20 June 1913. Mrs. Robert Heaven, the Countess of Carnwath and Miss Ekin would never be seen in eccentric fashions like those in No. 222, but are well dressed in a quiet way, and sufficiently fashionable to have ventured on the new 'low' V-necks.

225 Ascot 1914. Hobble-skirted dresses with tunics, fairly small hats, one with osprey feathers; the man in a morning suit.

226 Mr. and Mrs. Winston Churchill at the Hendon air pageant, 1914. Mr. Churchill in a dark lounge suit and square crowned hat; Mrs. Churchill wearing an exaggerated swathed hobble skirt tied in below the knee.

Beards

227 W. G. Grace, by Herbert Barraud, 1887. Full beard.

228 John Tyndall, by Herbert Barraud, 1888. Fringe beard and whiskers.

229 Hans von Bülow, by E. Bieber, Berlin, *c.* 1890. Goatee beard.

230 Emile Zola, by Paul Nadar, *c.* 1895. Normal beard.

Whiskers

231 Thomas H. Huxley, by A. G. Dew Smith, *c.* 1885. Dundrearies.

232 An old gentleman with sidewhiskers, *c.* 1857.

Moustaches

233 Napoleon III, by Mayer frères, 1854. Long waxed moustache.

234 Kaiser Wilhelm II, 1889. 'Kaiser moustache'.

235 A French orchestra at a gramophone recording session, *c.* 1905. Not one lacks a moustache.

PREFACE

I have often been disconcerted by the absence of dates on paintings in art museums. Dates of birth and death of the artist provide inadequate guidance, leaving the visitor to guess as to whether he sees an early or a late work. Apart from stylistic differences indicating the artist's development, which are frequently known to the expert, a study of costume and hair styles would enable most paintings to be at least approximately dated.

In forming our photo-historical collection, it was immediately apparent to my husband and me that old photographs ought to be dated as accurately as possible. This information adds to their significance and is invaluable to the historian. In doing research on early photographs, which are seldom dated, I soon found it essential to be able to recognize the style of dress when people appear in the picture. Even as a child I had always enjoyed the costumes in Shakespeare's and other historical plays, and one of my ambitions was to play the harp wearing a trained gown swirled round my feet and long draperies hanging gracefully from my bare arms. This romantic conception of dress tended to make me allergic to short-skirted modern fashions, and more interested in those of the past. It was with pleasure, therefore, that some fifteen years ago I began compiling descriptions of the fashions of each year from the official introduction of photography in 1839. This information I augmented with rough sketches based on fashion-plates in the journals I studied. Not infrequently, exactly dated photographs puzzled me, until I realized that people sometimes gave favourite old portraits to friends, writing on them the date of presentation. Publishers, too, often issued portraits of celebrities taken several years earlier.

It is fascinating to see the extent to which the reality as shown in photographs differs from the ideal images of fashion-plates. Royalty (when young), actresses and society beauties achieved a close approximation to fashion-plates. Other well-to-do people, on the other hand, though usually conforming with the main trend of fashion, sometimes showed modifications of it, and a few created styles of their own, which in the days of private dressmakers were not difficult to put into effect.

Old photographs illustrate not only the clothes people wore, but also reveal their attitudes, their way of sitting or standing, how they draped a shawl, held a sunshade or muff, or took off a top hat. According to fashion-plates, women had a drooping attitude in the 1840s, were stiffly upright in the 'eighties, whilst in the early Edwardian period they seem to be bending backward and forward at the same time. Photographs reveal these attitudes to a less marked degree, and the proportion that do is small. The historian of fashion relying solely on the fantasies of fashion-plates and painted portraits stresses the exception rather than the general trend as shown in the majority of photographs, which alone provide convincing proof of what people really did wear. Similarly, an historian of the future relying exclusively on press photographs of the startling models of a few leading fashion houses, which create a sensation each season, would altogether miss the real appearance of well-dressed people.

In my research I consulted, in addition to fashion magazines, innumerable costume books. Most were illustrated with fashion-plates and other graphic art, and only a small number also contained a few contemporary photographs. So I decided on the novelty of a book illustrated entirely with old photographs, to demonstrate what fashion looked like in reality. Since the idea of this book is to show *fashion*, the photographs chosen are, with certain exceptions, of upper and middle class people. I dislike using these terms but they are unavoidable in this context, for this period of the first threequarters of a century of photography shows women in an enormous variety of clothes suitable only for a lady of leisure. Full, heavy skirts, restricting corsets, vast crinolines, bustles, hampering tied-back skirts, long trains, hobble skirts — in each decade they underline women's inactivity, which made possible such fantasies of dress.

All this disappeared with the Great War and the long-overdue emancipation of women which was part of the new structure of society that emerged from it. Clothes became, and have remained, fairly practical and comfortable, with one outstanding exception: the fetish of the high heel. It increased until its present extreme height and narrowness surpasses anything known before. It is understandable that women may endure such shoes at an occasional party, but I am filled with amazement when I see young mothers pushing a perambulator in the park, and women doing their domestic shopping, staggering on stiletto heels with bent knees. Of course, many go by car nowadays and do little walking, but the first thing they do when they feel they can relax is to take their shoes off. I have even seen girls carrying their stiletto-heeled shoes in the dignified halls of art museums.

The uniformity and comparative lack of variety in men's clothes as compared with women's has naturally led me to include more photographs of the latter. Since before the introduction of photography men have been wearing plain cloth suits consisting of long trousers, coat or jacket, and a waistcoat more or less fanciful according to period. Cut, length, width and details of these garments have varied, of course, but in fundamental principle there has been far less change in men's clothes than in women's. The clothes of Victorian men do not look so utterly strange by present-day standards as those of women and children. If we saw a woman wearing a crinoline we would guess from afar that she was probably taking part in a film, but a man in clothes of the same period might pass as an eccentric.

According to the social historian Max von Boehn,[1] male clothing in the nineteenth century realized two of the slogans of the first French Revolution — equality and fraternity. After the silk, lace and embroidery of the old régime, sober cloth garments became a symbol of democracy and an outward equalizer utterly unknown in any earlier period. Men's clothes became practically a uniform. There remained, of course, distinctions in quality and cut, style of shirt and tie, and in the correctness of the clothes for a particular occasion, so that Polonius' advice to Laertes : 'the apparel oft proclaims the man' still held good.

In contrast to the sombreness of male attire, Victorian and Edwardian women had no inhibitions about using rich silks and elaborate trimmings even in the daytime. These were not considered to give an overdressed appearance, as they would today except for formal evening wear. The feminine aim in dress was perhaps more than today, to look attractive in *all* circumstances, and I believe the photographs in this book show that many succeeded. Their complicated clothes fitted perfectly, and during the greater part of the period defects of figure could be successfully disguised by full skirts or some form of drapery. The narrow vertical lines of modern dress, on the contrary, are becoming only to the slim hipless figure.

In the early years of photography, pictures of people were of necessity static in effect owing to the need to keep still during the exposure. With the daguerreotype and Calotype process during the 1840s and early 'fifties it might last a minute — varying greatly with lighting conditions and plate size. The faster wet collodion process introduced in 1851 made it possible for small stereoscopic and *carte-de-visite* portraits to be taken in a few seconds, but large studio portraits required much longer exposures. Only after the general introduction of the still more sensitive gelatine dry plate about 1880 was it possible to take real action-shots.

The photographs in this book may, I hope, be found useful by stage and film designers in re-creating the Victorian and Edwardian clothes which I so

[1] Max von Boehn, *Vom Kaiserreich zur Republik.* Berlin, 1917.

Preface

much admire. They will doubtless also prove of value to social historians, and indeed all students of the nineteenth century.

The Bibliography and Study List includes certain books more concerned with the philosophy of dress, or social conditions, than with fashion. I have listed their titles, assuming that some of my readers may wish to study the subject in its widest aspects.

ALISON GERNSHEIM
LONDON

PART I

The Rise and Fall of the Crinoline

W hen Queen Victoria came to the throne in 1837, the trend which was later to culminate in that characteristic Victorian feminine fashion, the crinoline, had already been under way some fifteen years — ever since the narrow-skirted high-waisted Regency gowns began to give place to a waistline at natural height and skirts widening at the hem. The romantic fashions of the 1830 period with balloon sleeves, comparatively short 'ballet dancer's' skirts, upstanding 'giraffe' hair style and flamboyant hats underwent a complete change of spirit by the time of the young Queen's accession, as though welcoming the new bourgeois ideal.

Never before or since has Western women's costume expressed respectability, acquiescence and dependence to such a degree as in the 1840s, the most static decade in nineteenth-century fashion. In retrospect, female costume of the 'forties seems stereotyped in form, and even contemporary fashion journalists found little new to report beyond details of trimming.

Characteristics of the period are a tight-fitting pointed bodice (1, 6, 8, 9, 12, 14, 16), and long full skirt gauged or pleated into a dome form, and supported by a small crescent-shaped bustle and innumerable petticoats. Contrary to fashion plates and descriptions, photographs belie the supposedly extremely long bodice.

Out of doors, particularly, the ubiquitous poke-bonnet and shawl or mantle produced a peculiarly respectable appearance. It is difficult to visualize the dashing *lionnes* of Paris society, the charming midinettes of Henri Murger, the disreputable *belles* of the Opera balls, and international adventuresses like Lola Montez, wearing such demure garments. Drawings by Gavarni and other caricaturists in the 'forties depict females in decidedly questionable situations, who nevertheless look like prudes.

The prevailing impression is one of severity, despite beautiful silks and dainty trimmings, and of primness even in *décolletée* ball dresses, for the

25

seductiveness of the exceedingly low and wide neckline is contradicted by the stiffness of the bertha and armoured effect of the boned bodice.

In outdoor costume, women were shut in and protected. The poke-bonnet projected so far that the face could only be seen from directly in front, and the enveloping shawl or mantle made even young girls look quite middle-aged in figure. Women seemed to be trying to hide in their clothes. Feet and limbs — as the unmentionable legs were referred to — were hidden by the skirt, sleeves entirely covered the arms, hands were seldom ungloved even indoors, and the bonnet not only shielded the face but had a *bavolet* or curtain covering the back of the neck (No. 4, 10). People would criticize a plain, large-featured woman: 'You can see her nose beyond her bonnet.'[1]

Although silks, lace, flowers, feathers and ringlets produced a charming effect, yet there was at the same time an aura of forbidden fruit. Dress was, as always, an expression of woman's place in society.

Fashion was created in Paris — but it was the Paris of Louis-Philippe, who was laughed at for carrying a big *bourgeois* umbrella — in those days still a dowdy accessory. 'Those who do not wish to be taken as belonging to the vulgar herd', advised a Parisian snob, 'prefer to risk a wetting rather than be looked upon as pedestrians in the street, for an umbrella is a sure sign that one possesses no carriage.' To be sure, the Citizen King drove in a carriage, sitting between Queen Marie-Amélie and his sister Madame Adelaide, who bravely tried to hide him with their large bonnets, as a protection against assassination attempts, of which there were seven in his reign. Immediately after such attacks, society women would call at the Tuileries to offer the King their congratulations, wearing clothes which they kept at hand for these alarming occasions. They were known as 'costumes for days on which the King's life is attempted' and were simple in form and dark in hue.[2] Normally, colours were mixed in a way that sounds shocking when we read the descriptions, but it must be realized that the delicate shades of the vegetable dyes were carefully harmonized, and bright colours frowned upon as vulgar. A fashion magazine[3] describes a public promenade dress of pea-green silk worn under a three-quarter-length pelisse-mantle of lavender and pink shot taffeta trimmed with Mechlin lace, and a blue taffeta redingote worn with a pink crape [*sic*] *chapeau* covered with embroidered tulle and trimmed with sprigs of roses. A pink *barège* carriage dress was worn with a green taffeta half-length mantle and a straw bonnet trimmed with two red and four white roses, with their foliage.

[1] Isabel Cooper-Oakley, 'History of Bonnets in Queen Victoria's Reign' in *The Woman's World*, August 1888.
[2] Augustin Challamel, *The History of Fashion in France*, London, 1882.
[3] *The Monthly Belle Assemblée*, June 1847.

Other bonnets had wreaths of grapes, cherries, and red currants. These were summer bonnets of Leghorn or rice straw, or silk. For winter, velvet or satin was the correct material, and ostrich feather tips replaced flowers or fruit as trimming.

In the 1840s all bonnets, indoor caps (Nos. 1, 6, 21), and evening head-dresses came down low at the sides of the face. Bonnet brims almost met beneath the chin, and were often lined with gauged or gathered net or tulle, and trimmed with flowers inside the brim, framing the face — a pretty fashion that lasted many years. This type of 'drawn' bonnet was worn by Dorothy Draper when she sat to her brother Dr. John Draper of New York in summer 1840 (No. 3). It is one of the first successful daguerreotype portraits, and the earliest to survive until modern times. Miss Draper wears a pelerine or shoulder cape of transparent muslin and her dress has 'Victoria' sleeves with puffs on the upper arm. During that summer long tight sleeves began to come in, and were general by the autumn. These 'Amadis' sleeves were cut with two seams like those of a man's coat, and were curved to the exact shape of the arm. By 1841 tight sleeves were almost universal and were set in so low at the shoulder (Nos. 1, 6, 8, 16 etc.) — often headed by a *mancheron* (later called jockey) — that the wearer could scarcely raise her arms. Five years later sees the tentative beginnings of shorter sleeves widening to reveal a false white undersleeve or *engageante* (No. 24) — a type of sleeve worn until the mid-'sixties.

Silk fabrics of all kinds were the main materials for dresses, even in the morning. In Paris shop girls, midinettes, seamstresses and artificial flower makers made great efforts to possess at least one silk dress — like the girls in Henri Murger's novel *La Vie de Bohême*. Striped Pekin silks, checks, plaid, chameleon or shot silk in changing colours, small printed patterns, and plain colours were all worn.

Jupons de crinoline are mentioned as early as July 1840. These petticoats lined with stiff horsehair cloth (Latin *crinis* – hair, *linum* – linen) were recommended as being 'very light and cool, and make the dress sit beautifully'.[1] From this time onward, therefore, it is not entirely incorrect to speak of the crinoline, though it is usual to reserve this designation for the separate metal-cage crinoline introduced in 1856.

Trailing skirts gave rise to the story that the municipal authorities found it an unnecessary expense to employ street cleaners for doing what ladies so kindly performed *gratis*. The inventor of this joke overlooked the fact that ladies seldom walked. For those who did, a *châtelaine* in the form of a negro's head on a chain to fasten up the skirt was introduced in the mid-'forties.

---

[1] *The Court Magazine & Monthly Critic & Ladies' Magazine & Museum of the Belles Lettres, Music, Fine Arts, Drama, Fashion, etc.,* July 1840.

The Rise and Fall of the Crinoline

To modern eyes there is not a great difference in general form between travelling and walking dress as compared with visiting or carriage toilets: the distinction lay chiefly in the material and trimming. In one's garden or on a country outing, a broad-brimmed Gipsy Leghorn hat (No. 12) might be worn instead of a bonnet, if a parasol were not wanted. 1841 saw the introduction of an arrangement of pleats, folds, or trimming from the sloping shoulders to the point of the waist, called *revers en pelerine* (Nos. 1, 6, 9, 23 etc.), and in the 'fifties, *bretelles* (No. 34). Day dresses in the early 'forties usually had a plain skirt, occasionally with one or two wide flounces (No. 7) at the bottom. From 1843 onward flounces became increasingly in evidence, and were sometimes scalloped or pinked at the edges. The neckline in summer for day dresses was quite often low (Nos. 8, 9, 12, 14); in winter higher, or closed with a *chemisette* (No. 16).

A typical ball dress might have a double or triple skirt — the upper ones being shorter and giving the effect of deep flounces — of white or pale-coloured thin material such as net or tarlatan, a new textile in 1840. A more solid material such as satin formed the foundation skirt and the tight bodice with deep points at the back and front. If the skirt were single, it would have applied decoration of *passementerie* (fancy braid) or lace flounces. The neckline was very low from shoulder to shoulder and cut either straight across with a bertha or flat flounce in mid-seventeenth-century style, or with a dip in the middle of the front, in which case there were folds of material arranged *à la grecque*. The short sleeves were usually hidden beneath the bertha or drapery. Boots for evening sound incongruous, but they were dainty objects of white or coloured silk.

For balls and other full-dress occasions the hair was decorated with artificial flowers matching the small tight round bouquet of real ones. With evening dress (which we would call dinner dress) a variety of turbans, Renaissance berets, and other *coiffures historiques* were the correct head-dress in the first half of the 'forties; in the later years of the decade, a wreath was preferred (No. 21).

Little girls' hair was done in long ringlets (No. 2) and side curls *à la Sévigné* were worn by grown-up women (Nos. 9, 13), especially in the evening, but there was always the alternative of loops or plaits of hair in front of the ears (Nos. 1, 14, 16 etc.). Towards the end of the decade these began to supersede curls, but women with naturally curly hair clung to their ringlets, as Elizabeth Barrett Browning did. The hair was parted in the middle, and arranged at the back in a projecting basket shape of plaits. The style came very close to that of the mid-seventeenth century, except for the absence of small curls on the forehead. The centre parting was practically obligatory; it was unthinkable that it could be anywhere else. Since this is where thinning of the hair usually begins in women, the customary indoor cap was no doubt welcomed with relief by those no longer young. But even the young and fashionable woman was supposed to wear a cap as soon as she had children. In fact, such indoor caps were fashionable, and not matronly as they seem to us. In 1844 a lace cap from Paris called the *bonnet assassin* was said to live up to its name and 'makes a tolerably pretty woman look very killing'. However, examination of photographs shows that the cap was not so universal as fashion writers claimed (No. 8). The same applies to the short white or yellow kid gloves which fashion articles and books on etiquette insisted must be constantly worn except at meals, and even *en négligée*.

Gradually bonnets became smaller and the brim opening changed from a vertical oval in the first half of the 'forties (No. 1, 4, 7) to a circular outline at the end (No. 19, 24). Up to 1845 the crown and brim had a perceptible join; thereafter, bonnets were made in one piece in a horizontal 'coalscuttle' form.

Necklaces were returning to favour, and hair bracelets *d'amitié* were popular for several decades (No. 46). A bracelet containing a watch was a novelty in 1844. 'The dial plate is covered by a cameo or enamelled case, with a cypher in diamonds. By touching a spring, a lady can always know the hour, and she can do that behind her fan without being observed.'[1] In those days it would have been rude to look openly at a wristwatch, giving an impression of boredom.

As in former centuries, a rather large lace-edged handkerchief was carried as a decorative accessory. Such a handkerchief can be seen in many of the paintings of Queen Victoria throughout her reign. Lace was highly prized at this period. The Honiton lace for the Queen's wedding dress in 1840 cost £1000, and by the end of her reign she is said to have possessed lace worth £76,000. Her collection was exceeded only by that of a man : the Pope's lace was valued at £200,000.[2]

The most popular winter furs were sable and ermine, especially for muffs, but fancy muffs of material were used more than those of fur alone. Swansdown was worn instead of fur in spring and autumn.

In the summer tiny sunshades were carried, often of the hinged type invented in the eighteenth century and illustrated by Gillray in 1795. Often a *canezou* — a kind of sleeveless blouse of lace or muslin — was worn over the dress. Even in hot weather some kind of outdoor garment was added; though it might be of lace (No. 10), it was felt to give the correct finish for outdoor clothes.

---

[1] *The New Monthly Belle Assemblée*, 1844.
[2] Octave Uzanne, *Fashion in Paris*, London, 1898.

Pardessus was the general term for an immense variety of half or threequarter length wraps, mantles, mantlets, *visites*, pelisses and other garments which look all rather alike to us. In the early 'forties, all but the polonaise were loose, but in the latter part of the decade many outdoor wraps fitted at the waist.

The first half of the nineteenth century saw the apotheosis of the shawl of oriental origin which became fashionable in Europe through Napoleon's Egyptian campaign in 1798, when officers sent home Eastern shawls as presents. Josephine had between 300 and 400 shawls, some of them worth as much as 12,000 francs (£500).

In its country of origin, Cashmere, the shawl was a gift of princes in return for the offerings of their vassals; the word shawl means gift. Cashmere shawls were made of the finest, most delicate wool in the entire world — that of the Tibetan goat. The method of forming it into complicated patterns by a combination of needle- and loom-work remained the secret of a few native families. The production of a pair of shawls — two identical shawls were always made together — took several years.[1]

In Europe, methods of production on hand-looms were invented in Lyons, Rheims, Norwich, Bradford and Huddersfield, but only the factory at Paisley near Glasgow came close to the quality of the originals. Queen Victoria lent the Paisley mill her Cashmere shawls as patterns. Under the Treaty of Lahore, 9 March 1846, by which Cashmere was ceded to Britain, the Maharajah Gholab Singh as tributary sovereign sent Queen Victoria an annual tribute of one horse, twelve shawl-goats, and three pairs of shawls.

The characteristic pattern of Cashmere shawls is the pine or cone — the male or pollen-bearing organ of the date-palm, which occurs in many oriental designs.[2] Animal-headed gods carved in relief on the walls of the Assyrian King Ashurnasirpal III's palace at Nimrud (9th century B.C.) hold such cones, representing the manual transference of pollen to the female or date-bearing tree. The symbolism presumably remained unknown to early-Victorian wives, and one can only speculate as to whether their large families could be attributed to the influence of the fertility emblems on their shawls!

The fashion for Paisley shawls (No. 27) lasted well into the 'sixties, by which time they had become a common mass-produced article, sometimes even printed, not woven. But even as late as 1887 genuine Cashmere shawls of top quality were sold in London at £100 to £400 each.[3]

It was said that a fine shawl could be drawn through a wedding ring, and doubtless a light-weight shawl was more convenient in changeable summer

[1] Matthew Blair, *The Paisley Shawl*, Paisley 1904.   [2] ibid.   [3] *The Lady's World*, 1887.

weather than a coat with sleeves, which cannot be carried so easily. As for our cardigans, the less said about them the better.

In the 'forties there was little difference in the dress of a girl over the age of seven or eight and her mother's; the shortness of the frock and the addition of pantaloons was all that distinguished it. Ankle-length white pantaloons or 'trowsers' (later called drawers) for girls came in before 1820 and lasted for nearly forty years (No. 56). Sometimes they were shams consisting of two separate tubes tied on at the knee, the purpose being merely to hide the legs. Children wore white stockings and half-boots more often than shoes.

A boy of fourteen is shown in a fashion-plate of 1844 in clothes exactly like a grown-up man's, complete with top hat. Up to the age of six boys wore a frock like a girl's.

In the following decade girls continued to be dressed like adults apart from their pantaloons (Nos. 38, 56). Small boys (there is one earnestly studying the globe in No. 29) can hardly be distinguished from their sisters except by their shorter hair. (Little Lord Fauntleroy curls came later.) Slightly older boys wore long checked trousers like their fathers', short dark jacket, light waistcoat, and sometimes a military looking peaked cap (No. 35). The Highland dress was popularized in France as well as in England by the visit of the thirteen-year-old Prince of Wales to Paris in 1855, and was sometimes worn by the young Prince Imperial.

Considering the number of underclothes, the tight corsets, the boned bodice with back-fastenings of hooks and eyes, the restricting sleeves, and the weight of petticoats, it seems strange that women's dress should be praised for its convenience. Only lack of personal experience could have given rise to this opinion, which I am therefore inclined to attribute to a man. 'The female attire of the present day is, upon the whole, in as favourable a state as the most vehement advocates for what is called Nature and simplicity could desire. It is a costume in which they can dress quickly, walk nimbly, eat plentifully, stoop easily, loll gracefully; and in short, perform all the duties of life without let or hindrance. . . . Nor is the ankle even hopeless, if you are sufficiently attentive, and if it be worth showing.'[1]

Balzac had already observed that a woman's dress is 'a permanent revelation of her most secret thoughts, a language and a symbol'[2] and this Englishman shared his up-to-date ideas on the psychology of clothes, feeling, as we do, that 'Dress is a sort of symbolical language, the study of which it would be madness to neglect. To a proficient in the science, every woman walks about with a placard on which her leading qualities are advertised. . . . Upon the whole, a

[1] *The Quarterly Review*, March 1847.   [2] Honoré de Balzac, *Une Fille d'Eve*, 1839.

prudent and sensible man may safely predicate of the inner lining from the outer garment, and be thankful that he has this, at least, to go by.'[1] Aware of the fallacy of such deductions if applied without discrimination, the writer is quick to add : 'Of all the various denominations of swindlers, that woman is the basest, who is a dandy during courtship and a dowdy after marriage. We should doubt whether the woman who is indifferent to her own appearance be a woman at all. At all events, she must be either a hardened character, or an immense heiress, or a first-rate beauty — or think herself one.'

'An old woman nowadays literally does not know how to dress herself. Why are we tried with the unbecoming appearance of those who won't be old and can't be young? She who is ashamed to wear a costume as old as herself, may rely upon it she only looks older than her costume' (Nos. 21, 25). Mutton dressed up as lamb is rarely seen today, except in the case of a certain type of elderly dame from America, addicted to heavily flowered hats and 'jewelled' hairnets in the daytime.

'The male costume is reduced to a mysterious combination of the inconvenient and the unpicturesque', complains the same writer, not without justification, 'hot in summer — cold in winter — stiff without being plain — bare without being simple — not durable, not becoming, and not cheap. No single article is left in his wardrobe with which he can even make what is called an impression — a conquest is out of the question. Each taken separately is as absurd as the emptiest fop could have devised, and as ugly as the staunchest Puritan could have desired. The hat is a machine to which an impartial stranger might impute a variety of useful culinary purposes, but would never dream of putting on his head. His stock looks like a manicle with which he has escaped from prison, or his cravat like a lasso with which he has been caught in the act. His stiff collars may be entitled to their name of *Vatermörder* in Germany,[2] but certainly never did any other execution there or elsewhere.'

These *Vatermörder* or 'parricides' were the tall upstanding collar with two points projecting on the cheeks (Nos. 5, 18, 20, etc.) — a moderate version of the still higher collar which had been in fashion from the beginning of the century. Young men like the Hamburg artists in No. 11 mostly wore collars of a new type, turning outward over the neckcloth, which was tied in a bow in front. Another type of cravat was tied in a barrel-knot (No. 22) whilst the scarf cravat completely covered the shirt-front (No. 17).'La cravate c'est l'homme', declared Balzac, for the art of tying a cravat well was the mark of a gentleman.

---

[1] *The Quarterly Review*, March 1847.
[2] The name is derived from the legend of a student who returned from the university wearing such a stiff collar that on embracing his father it cut the old gentleman's throat.

2 *The Grierson sisters. Calotype by D. O. Hill and R.*
   Adamson, Edinburgh, c. 1845

1 *Mrs. Napier. Calotype by David Octavius Hill and Robert*
   Adamson, Edinburgh, c. 1845

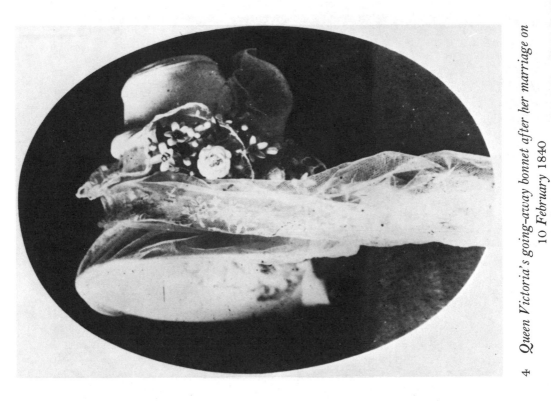

4 *Queen Victoria's going-away bonnet after her marriage on 10 February 1840*

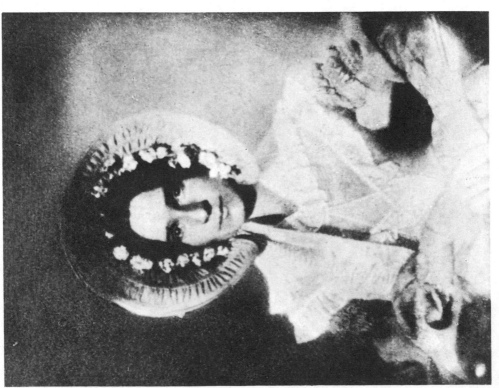

3 *Miss Dorothy Draper. Daguerreotype by Prof. John W. Draper, Summer 1840*

6　A lady. Daguerreotype by A. Schwendler, Dresden, c. 1844

5　W. H. Fox Talbot, inventor of the Calotype process of photography. Daguerreotype by A. Claudet, 1844

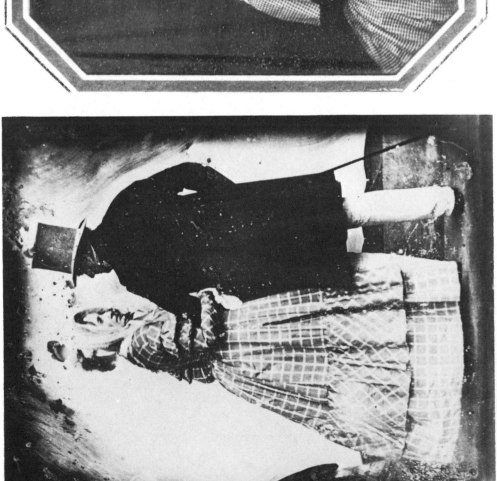

8 *Fräulein Reimer, Frau Stelzner, Fräulein Mathilde von Braunschweig. Daguerreotype by C. F. Stelzner. Hamburg, c. 1842*

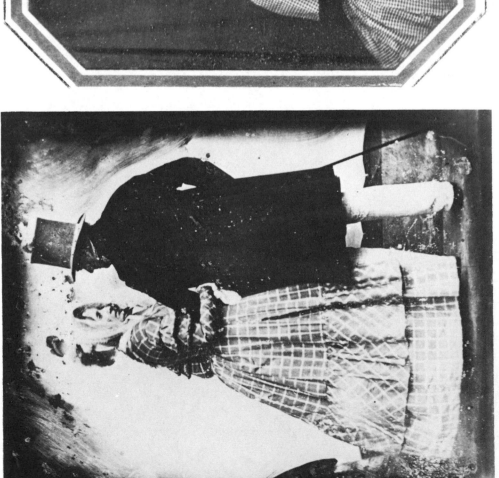

7 *Lady in checked dress. Daguerreotype. Prague, c. 1842*

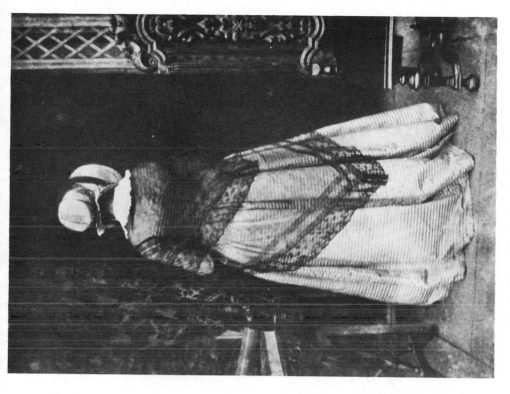

10 *Lady Mary Ruthven. Calotype by D. O. Hill and*
    R. Adamson, Edinburgh, c. 1845

9 *David Octavius Hill and the Misses Morris. Calotype by*
   Robert Adamson, Edinburgh, 1843–45

11 *An outing of the Hamburg Artists' Club, May 1843*

13 *Miss Chalmers and her brother. Calotype by D. O. Hill and
R. Adamson, Edinburgh, c. 1843*

12 *Miss McCandlish. Calotype by D. O. Hill and
R. Adamson, Edinburgh, c. 1843*

15 *A gentleman. Daguerreotype attributed to Richard Beard, London, c. 1845*

14 *A lady. Daguerreotype. Milan, c. 1845*

17　*A gentleman. Daguerreotype, c. 1845*

16　*A lady with a reading-glass. Daguerreotype by A. Claudet, London, c. 1843*

19   *A lady. Daguerreotype by J. E. Mayall, London,*
     c. 1849

18   *A gentleman. Daguerreotype by E. Kilburn, London,*
     c. 1850

21　*A lady. Daguerreotype by William Telfer, London, c.* **1848**

20　*Gioachino Rossini. Daguerreotype, Paris, c.* **1852**

22 *A gentleman. Daguerreotype by Howie, Edinburgh, c. 1845*

23 *Baroness de Späth. Daguerreotype by A. Claudet, London, 1852*

24   *A lady. Daguerreotype by William Telfer, London, c. 1849*

25   *A lady. Daguerreotype by A. Claudet, London, c. 1853*

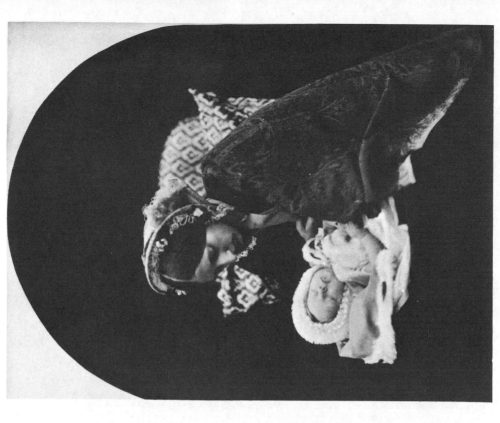

27 *Eleanor Cooper and baby, by George Cooper. 1856*

26 *Young girl in riding habit, c. 1855*

29   *The Geography Lesson. Stereoscopic daguerreotype
by A. Claudet, London, 1851*

28   *At the ball, c. 1853*

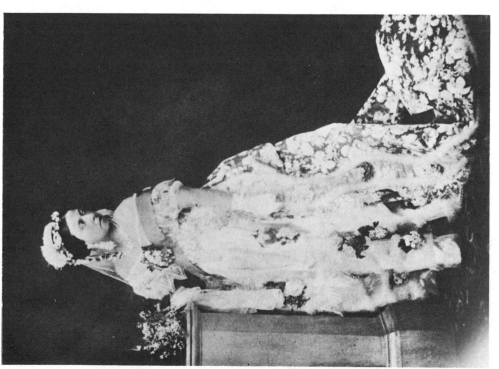

30 *Queen Victoria in Court dress after a Drawing-room at Buckingham Palace on 11 March 1854. By Roger Fenton.*

31 *Prince Albert, by J. E. Mayall, Osborne, August 1855*

33   *David Octavius Hill and his sister Mary Watson,
Edinburgh, c. 1858*

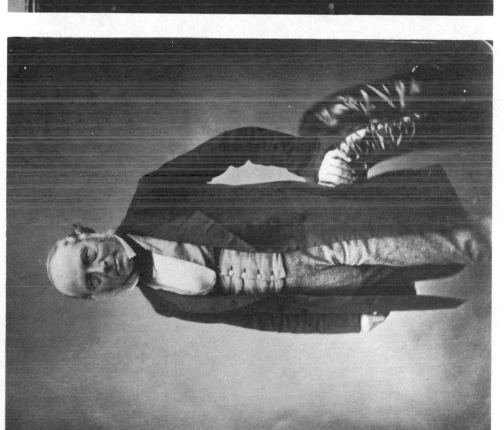

32   *Sir Rowland Hill, by Maull & Polyblank, London, c. 1858*

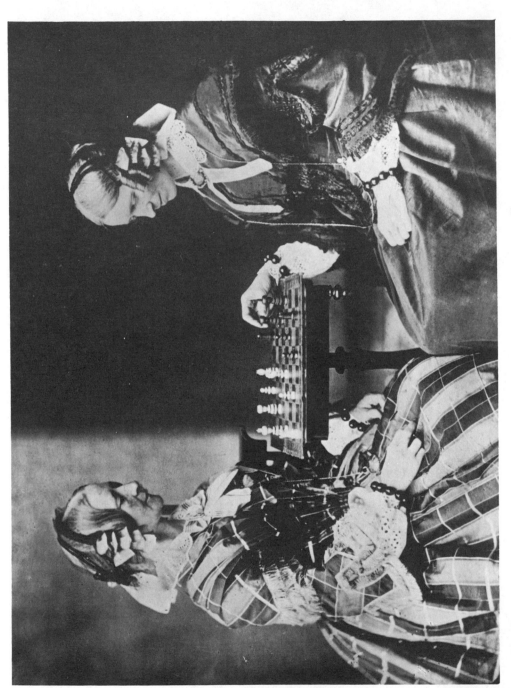

34　*The Misses Lutwidge playing chess, by Lewis Carroll, c. 1857*

36   *A little girl. Daguerreotype by Anson, New York, 1855*

35   *Prince Alfred, the tutor F. W. Gibbs, and the Prince of Wales, by Roger Fenton, Windsor, 8 February 1854*

38   *The Misses Dingwall-Fordyce of Brucklay Castle,*
by G. W. Wilson, Aberdeen, c. 1858

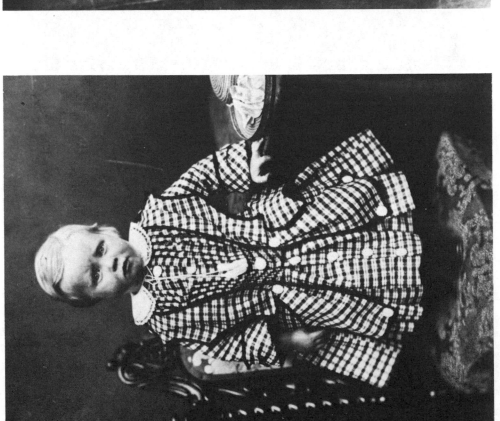

37   *George Wilson, by G. W. Wilson, Aberdeen, 1857*

39 *Mrs. Fisher, by G. W. Wilson, Aberdeen, c. 1857*

40 *Sir Archibald Alison, by Maull & Polyblank, London, c. 1858*

41   *Young lady by Maull & Polyblank, London, c. 1857*

42   *An unusually lively portrait for 1856*

44 *Princesses Helena and Louise, by Roger Fenton, c. 1857*

43 *Mother and daughter, 1858*

45 *A group photographed at Osborne by Colonel D. F. de Ros, March 1858*

47   *Michael Faraday, by Maull & Polyblank, London, c. 1855*

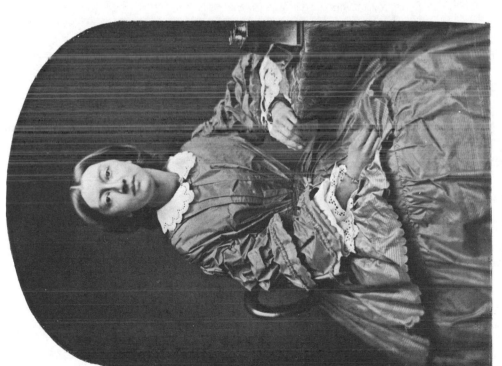

46   *Mrs. William Blake, c. 1854*

49 *Gentleman with tall top hat, c. 1858*

48 *Alfred Tennyson, by James Mudd, c. 1857*

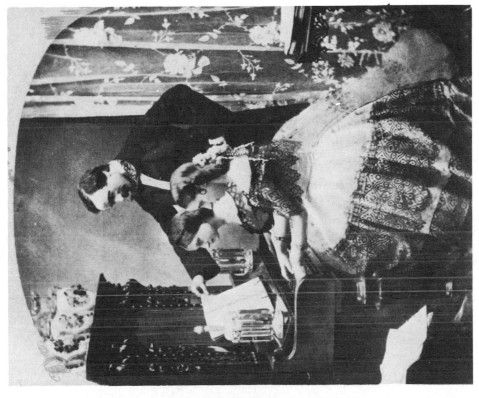

51　*The Duet, c.* 1357

50　*The Princess Royal (later the Empress Frederik of Germany) in her confirmation dress. Windsor, 20 March 1856. By W. Bambridge*

52 *Margate beach, c. 1858*

54 *Lord Brougham, by Maull & Polyblank, London, 1856*

53 *Miss Carr, c. 1860*

56 *Princess Marie of Hohenzollern-Sigmaringen, 1858*

55 *A crinoline shop in Paris, c. 1862*

58   *The Empress Eugénie, by Disdéri, Paris, 1859*

57   *Princess Frederick William of Prussia (the Princess Royal)*, 1 June 1859

59   Queen Victoria and the Prince Consort, by J. E. Mayall, 1861

60   Lady in dress of vertically striped material, c. 1862

The Rise and Fall of the Crinoline

From about 1848 onward excessively high collars and wide cravats gradually went out of fashion, but well on into the 'fifties old men were still wearing 'parricides'. The name cravat, incidentally, derives from *Croat*. During the Thirty Years' War officers of French troops fighting with the armies of Gustav Adolf of Sweden took a liking to the neckcloths of the Croatian troops in the service of the Emperor Ferdinand of Germany, and introduced them into France. The fashion reached England thirty years later with the restoration of Charles II.[1]

In the 1840s coats in dark shades of brown, green, and blue were still to be seen even in the evening, but by 1853 nineteen out of twenty dress coats were black. The swallow-tail dress coat with rectangular cut-in (No. 47) was worn on formal occasions in the daytime as 'half dress' until 1861 when it was relegated to the evening only. At formal evening parties in the 'forties pantaloons were still worn, but for ordinary evening wear and during the day, trousers were correct. Being rather tight, they sometimes had a strap passing beneath the boot or shoe to keep them down, until the 'fifties when they became looser.[2]

Light-coloured (No. 9) or checked (No. 17) suits with a short-skirted coat could be worn outside London, but for town wear the trend towards sombre hues — apart from the fancy waistcoat — had already set in. The dark frock coat, with skirt descending vertically to the knees, was the garment worn on most day-time occasions, and the top hat — black, white, or fawn — was the standard headgear (Nos. 5, 7, 11 etc.). Alfred de Musset had attacked the black suit as a horrid symbol of mourning for the illusions which human reason had destroyed.[3] It was the dullness of modern male attire that caused George Bernard Shaw's outburst in a lecture to amateur photographers: 'The nineteenth century — the most abominable century that ever existed — was the century in which people lost their love of colour. The nineteenth century got more and more afraid of colour, colour came to be looked upon as disreputable, and respectable men had to wear deep black and spotless white.'[4]

Men wore their hair moderately long, usually parted at the side, and curled forward in front of the ears (Nos. 15, 17, 20 etc.). From 1852 onward they greased it with Rowland's macassar oil — hence the need for antimacassars on the backs of chairs.[5] A moustache and whiskers, and even a thin fringe beard

[1] A. Varron, 'Neckties', *CIBA Review*, No. 38, 1941.

[2] C. W. & P. Cunnington, *Handbook of English Costume in the Nineteenth Century*, London 1959.

[3] Max von Boehn, *Die Mode: Menschen und Moden im neunzehnten Jahrhundert*, Vol. II, 1818–1842, 4th edition, Munich, n.d. (1919).

[4] *The Amateur Photographer*, 26 October 1909.

[5] From 1815 Alexander Rowland's macassar oil was used to promote the growth of the whiskers and eyebrows, but was not at that period applied to the hair.

under the chin (Nos. 22, 31) were not uncommon, but practically no beards were to be seen *on* the chin. On the Continent hair on the face was not only despised but politically suspect in the belief that only Republicans, Socialists and Radicals trying to disguise themselves would be unshaven. In 1846 Prussian postmen were forbidden to wear even a moustache. When Prince Louis Napoleon began to influence events in France after the Revolution of 1848, Thiers promised him his support, but urged him to shave off his moustache. Napoleon, however, considered this sacrifice too great, and later, as Emperor, grew his moustache until it was as long as Salvador Dali's, but waxed it outwards, however, not upwards (No. 233). In the early years of his reign the Emperor Franz Joseph of Austria forbade all state functionaries to wear beards, and in 1859, prior to Garibaldi's invasion of his kingdom, Francis II of Naples abolished beards by royal decree because 'they savour too much of the revolutionary principle of Garibaldi.'[1] In Naples a Frenchman was seized by the police and forcibly shaved in the nearest barber's shop. The Duke of Modena, too, ordered all male travellers whose passports were not in order to be shaved.[2]

In any clean-shaven period, of course, beards are considered outrageous on young men. At the time of the sensational Picasso exhibition at the Victoria & Albert Museum in 1946, a group of schoolboys — associating anything peculiar with that artist — surrounded my bearded husband in the street, yelling 'Picasso! Picasso!'

In the 1840s, many young Englishmen were clean-shaven, which aroused the ire of William Henry Henslowe, the bigoted author of a curious anonymous pamphlet entitled *Beard-Shaving, and the Common Use of the Razor, an unnatural, irrational, unmanly, ungodly, and fatal fashion among Christians* (1847). The fatality of this fashion was apparently the uncontrollable temptation to commit murder or suicide on seeing a razor left lying about — though surely a carving-knife on the dinner table might be considered equally dangerous to unbalanced characters. After citing Biblical texts against the shaving-off of beards, Henslowe quotes with satisfaction the *Sunday Times* of 21 February 1847: 'It is recently stated by a military (staff) surgeon, that *important physical advantages* are attached to mustachios. He says that they shelter the lips and strengthen the teeth, by resisting the influences of cold and heat. . . . By preserving an equal temperature about the skin, it protects the lips and the enamel of the teeth. Thus the teeth are rendered more serviceable for the biting

[1] Reginald Reynolds, *Beards: an omnium gatherum*, London 1950.
[2] Max von Boehn, *Die Mode: Menschen und Moden im neunzehnten Jahrhundert*, Vol. III, 1843–1878, 4th edition, Munich, n.d. (1919).

of cartridges; and the use of the mustachio is also a great saving in time at the soldier's toilet.'

In England, beards began to be worn in the 'fifties, particularly during the Crimean War, since it was not easy to shave in the camp before Sebastopol. *Punch* was already making fun of the beard and moustache movement in 1853, but a beard was still not quite respectable until the 'sixties, when it adorned the chins of a number of Members of both Houses of Parliament. Heavy side-whiskers were caricatured by the character of Lord Dundreary in Tom Taylor's play *Our American Cousin* (1861).

The etiquette of glove-wearing was strict. Count Alfred D'Orsay — called by *Le Charivari* 'King of the Dandies' — laid down the rule in 1839 that 'An English gentleman of fashion ought to use six pair of gloves a day:

'In the morning to drive a britzska to the hunt: Gloves of reindeer.

'At the hunt, to follow a fox: Gloves of shammy leather.

'To return to London in a Tilbury, after a drive at Richmond in the morning: Gloves of beaver.

'To go later for a walk in Hyde Park, or to conduct a lady to pay her visits or make her purchases in London, and *to offer her your hand in descending from the carriage:* Coloured kid Gloves braided.

'To go to a dinner-party: yellow dog's skin Gloves — and in the evening for a ball or rout: Gloves of white lamb-skin embroidered with silk.'[1]

Seven years later men were admonished to take an extra pair of gloves when invited to a dinner party. 'It may be that after dinner a dance will succeed, and no gentleman would ask a lady to confide her hand to gloves he had worn before dinner — the very idea is too indelicate to be tolerated; therefore cannot be too carefully guarded against.'[2] A man bathing naked (as was customary until the 1860s) in the Seine some distance from Paris was startled by frantic cries for help from an over-turned carriage. In this emergency he did not wait even to pick up a towel but rushed to the rescue of a young and charming woman who was trapped. 'Madame', he apologized, taking her hand to help her out, 'pardonnez-moi de n'avoir pas de gants.' Ladies were supposed to wear gloves indoors as well as out, except at meals.

In 1850 Landseer, Pickersgill, Leslie and other British artists denounced modern dress as 'devoid of all the requisites for dignified historic painting, utterly incongruous with sculpture, and no less unfavourable to the living figure'. In revolt against the top hat, artists, musicians, poets, and other 'Bohemians' usually wore a wide-brimmed soft felt hat with a low crown. It

---

[1] Octave Uzanne, *The Sunshade, the Glove, the Muff,* 1883.
[2] *The Ladies' Cabinet of Fashion,* 1846.

never occurred to anyone of any age or sex that headgear could be dispensed with altogether! This kind of hat, worn by Louis Kossuth, the Hungarian nationalist, became the badge of revolutionaries in artistic fields as well. Liszt, to whom Wagner had given one, aroused the suspicion of the police when he arrived at Karlsruhe in 1853 wearing a 'democratic hat'. Within a few years, however, it had become respectable enough in the stiffer form known as a wide-awake, for Prince Albert (No. 31) and the Poet Laureate (No. 48).

Fancy waistcoats were still worn except on formal occasions, when they had to be black. They were checked, striped, or tartan, and sometimes had large lapels (Nos. 31, 33, 35, 59). In the first half of the 'fifties the waistcoat and trousers were often of the same material and the coat different; and in the second half of the decade, coat and trousers might match and the waistcoat be of different material. Photographs show that there was no hard and fast rule about the combination (Nos. 42, 49).

Trousers were now wider and sometimes braided down the side seams (No. 54); they had no crease until the 'nineties. For day wear plaids, checks and stripes were much worn. Mrs. C. S. Peel relates that Lord Brougham when inspecting a weaving mill ordered two pieces of black and white check tweed. When the stuff was delivered he found there were 50 yards in each piece — enough to last for the rest of his life[1] (No. 54). Lord Brougham obviously did not mind sticking to the same style, for in this photograph of 1856 he was still wearing the 'parricide' tall stand-up collar that had been the fashion when he defended Queen Caroline in 1820 — and even earlier.

The morning coat introduced in the first half of the 'fifties was developed from the Newmarket or riding coat. The skirt was cut away from the waist in a gradual curve (Nos. 31, 35) towards the tails. The more formal frock coat had a skirt extending vertically to the knees, and the double-breasted type was called a 'Prince Albert' (Nos. 32, 33, 45). With both the morning coat and the frock coat a top hat was worn.

The man about town needed four morning coats, a frock coat for formal occasions, a dress tail coat for evening, and an overcoat. These seven coats, renewed every year, cost him about £18. Six pairs of morning and one pair of black evening trousers cost £9; four morning and one evening waistcoat £4. Gloves, linen, hats, scarves and neckties amounted to about £10, and boots at least £5 more.[2]

A leading tailor deplored the fact that black frock coats were sometimes to be

[1] Mrs. C. S. Peel, *The Stream of Time*, 1931.
[2] *The Habits of Good Society*, n.d. (c. 1855). Anonymous handbook quoted by James Laver in *Taste and Fashion*, 1945.

seen at weddings. For such a festive occasion the frock coat should be made of blue, claret, or mulberry-coloured cloth, with or without a velvet collar, and worn with a white waistcoat and pale lavender trousers. This outfit was recommended for the bridegroom as well as the guests, whereas formerly the bridegroom had worn evening dress if the bride wore a long veil instead of a bonnet.[1]

The easy-fitting country suit of the 'forties (Nos. 9, 17) which was a forerunner of the lounge suit (apart from the fitted waist when buttoned up) was further developed as the 'Tweedside', originating in Scotland by 1857. At first rather long, it was soon made shorter and squarer in cut, until in spring 1859 these three-piece suits of checked or flecked material, with sack-like jacket fastening on the top button only, began to become popular with young men (No. 65). They were felt to be extremely casual, and were sometimes called 'lounging suits'. The shallow round hard hat designed by William Bowler was worn with them. For riding, a morning coat, trousers (with spurs!) and a top hat were correct.

The most usual neck-clothes were a fairly broad tie, and a much narrower one called the shoestring tie; both fastened with a bow in front. By this time the high collars of the first half of the century had disappeared. The low collars worn included the turn-down or double collar leaving only the front bow and ends of the tie visible.

The 'sixties witnessed a great development of informal clothes. 'Ease is now looked upon as the desideratum in all articles of dress, especially when required to be worn in the country.'[2] There were short square-cut lounge jackets with narrow high lapels; Tweedside suits with longer jackets, short 'reefer' and 'pea jackets' with trousers of different material, and black velvet lounge jackets worn with check trousers, as well as 'suits of "dittoes" ' — meaning coat, waistcoat and trousers (or knickerbockers) of the same material (No. 77). This applied not only to lounge suits, including Tweedsides, but also to the morning coat. Even the formal frock coat relaxed its tight waist, and in 1869 quite short frock coats appeared. About 1866 the top hat was reduced somewhat in height (No. 85 on left).

For shooting and other sports a morning coat or a lounge jacket was worn with knickerbockers and leggings, or the Norfolk 'blouse' or 'shirt' introduced in 1866 — actually a tweed jacket, made easy-fitting with big vertical pleats. Combined in 1869 with knickerbockers of the same material, the Norfolk suit was created. Even with these casual clothes, a white shirt with starched collar was essential.

[1] *The Gazette of Fashion* by Edward Minister & Son, London, 1 March 1861.
[2] ibid. 1 August 1861.

The Rise and Fall of the Crinoline

It is curious how often men's fashions start with sport and then become formal, before finally dying out. The late eighteenth-century riding coat with rectangular cut-in tails became the nineteenth-century 'half-dress' day coat and evening dress coat. Nowadays 'tails' are reserved for the most formal occasions. The cut-away morning coat, which a hundred years ago was suitable for riding, shooting, and the seaside (No. 52) is now only seen at functions such as big weddings, royal garden parties, and Ascot. The lounge suit, introduced for casual countrified comfort, has climbed the ladder of elegance and is worn at cocktail parties. It has already become too conventional for many kinds of summer holiday. The old frock coat with full long skirt, descending from the eighteenth century, was obsolete after the Great War.

Such a development from sporting to formal dress rarely occurs in women's fashions, which are usually quickly discarded, but the tailor-made demonstrated it in its metamorphosis into the modern more feminine version, which is now too formal for country wear.

Elias Moses & Son, City outfitters who claimed to have originated the ready-made clothing system, opened a shop in New Oxford Street in the 1850s and began to compete with West End tailors in making clothes to measure. Their highest price for a made-to-measure dress coat of best quality cloth was £2 15s 0d., whilst ready-made dress coats were supplied at prices ranging from 17s. to £2 6s. 0d. Frock coats cost slightly more: best quality ready-made £2 10s. 0d., made-to-measure £3 3s. 0d. Silk hats, superior quality, cost 5s., and ladies' kid boots could be had from 3s. 9d. upwards. Men's winter overcoats, such as the Albert cape 'made of the most approved waterproof materials, lined throughout and velvet collar' were advertised from 25s. to 75s. Circular or Spanish cloaks with black or coloured velvet facings cost £6 6s. 0d.

Moses & Son claimed to have customers in all classes from prince to peasant, though obviously they catered chiefly for the lower and middle classes. Outfits were advertised for emigrants to Australia and all other parts of the world for as little as £3 10s. 0d. and £6 10s. 0d. The most expensive ten guinea outfit consisted of the following items:

Black dress coat	Hat and cloth cap
Ditto vest	18 shirts
Ditto trousers	4 night shirts
Frock coat	Pair Wellington boots and shoes
Fancy vest	6 handkerchiefs
Ditto trousers	6 lbs. Marine soap
Fishing or shooting coat	Razor, shaving box, strop and glass

Knife, fork and plate
Mug, table and tea-spoon
Bed, pillow, and pair of blankets
2 pairs sheets

2 pillowcases
Comb and hairbrush
Strong sea chest[1]

Lady's outfit to Australia — 'if necessary, a lower outfit may be had' :

30 Long Cloth Chemises	*each*	1. 3.	to	2.	6.
18 ditto night dresses		2. 2.		4.	3.
18 ditto short ditto		1. 10.		3.	0.
18 ditto or cambric slips		4. 0.		8.	6.
12 ditto petticoats		1. 9.		4.	0.
4 Welch flannel ditto		4. 0.		7.	6.
1 dress improver[2]		1. 0.		4.	6.
6 Musquito drawers		2. 0.		3.	0.
18 Long Cloth drawers		1. 6.		2.	6.
3 flannel ditto		3. 10.		4.	6.
2 Merino Union dresses		7. 0.		11.	6.
30 night caps		3½.		3.	0.
36 cotton cambric pocket handkerchiefs		3¼.			8.
36 linen ditto ditto		6½.		2.	6.
48 towels		6			10.
36 pairs white cotton stockings		3½.		1.	0.
12 ditto Merino ditto		1 9		3 11	
2 coloured morning dressing gowns		7. 6.		10.	0.
1 white satin stripe ditto		9. 6.		12.	6.
1 flannel gown		12. 0.		20.	0.
6 pairs sheets		3. 3.		4.	0.
12 pillow cases		6.		8½.	

[1] E. Moses & Son, *Fashions for 1857*, London, n.d. (1856).
[2] A small crescent-shaped bustle.

It will be noticed that the man's wardrobe included outer garments, whilst the woman's was restricted to underclothes and household linen.

'The effect of dress is indeed of unquestionable importance' Moses rightly insisted. 'A perfectly suitable dress is a passport almost everywhere. Wealth or worth ill-attired is usually ill received. Amongst strangers, dress is the only criterion of a man's title to consideration. "A man's appearance", says Addison, "falls within the censure of any one that sees him; his parts and learning few are judges of." '[1]

Through the enterprise of firms like Moses & Son, and big drapers like Swan & Edgar, London's middle-class was better dressed than ever before. Women's cloaks and mantles could be bought off the peg, but dresses had to fit tightly so the bodice was made to measure, although the skirt might be bought ready-made. The Paris fashions worn by upper-class Englishwomen were copied by innumerable skilful small dressmakers. 'Fashion is extremely aristocratic in its tendencies,' explained Mrs. Merrifield. 'Every change emanates from the highest circles, who reject it when it has descended to the vulgar. No new form of dress was ever successful which did not originate among the aristocracy. From the ladies of the court, the fashions descend through all the ranks of society, until they at last die a natural death among the cast-off clothes of the housemaid.'[2] This dictum remained valid until after World War II. Recently it has been somewhat modified, owing perhaps to the increased spending power of young working people who are adventurous in launching, or at least taking up, new fashions — often from abroad — whilst the upper classes tend to be conservative.

Mrs. Merrifield sternly attacked the use of make-up: 'We violate the laws of nature when we seek to repair the ravages of time on our complexion by paint, when we substitute false hair for that which age has thinned or blanched, or conceal the change by dyeing our own grey hair.' Her objection was mainly on the grounds of deceitfulness. 'To do either is not only bad taste, but it is a positive breach of sincerity . . . it is *acting a lie* to all intents and purposes, and it ought to be held in the same kind of detestation as falsehood with the tongue.' In modern times there is no intention to deceive. Visible lipstick became permissible in the late 1920s, and today blue or green eye-shadow and a dark outline on the eyelids are often seen even in broad daylight.

During the 'fifties women abandoned the drooping self-effacing attitude of the 'forties. For one thing, they were no longer half hidden by the projecting

---

[1] E. Moses & Son, *Gossip on Dress*, London, 1863.
[2] Mary Philadelphia Merrifield, *Dress as a Fine Art*, London, 1854. (Reprinted from articles published the previous year.)

bonnet brim, which retreated from the face until by 1855 the front half of the head was exposed (No. 27). Since only scholarly 'strong-minded females' who strained their eyes reading small print wore dark glasses, sunshades were more and more used, though only of the daintiest and most unpractical design (No. 43).

When Kossuth came to New York in 1851 every shop sold his broad-brimmed style of hat adapted for women. The fashion reached Europe three years later. They were called 'seaside hats' (No. 52), and a thin cord was attached to the centre front of the brim, by means of which the hat was held on in windy weather. A hat was considered rather fast after the long reign of the meek bonnet, and only dashing young women wore them. In Germany such a hat was called *letzter Versuch* — the last attempt of spinsters. An adequate brim on a bonnet would have been intolerably old-fashioned, and instead, a kind of screen known as an Ugly was attached to shade the eyes. Uglies were usually worn by elderly women (No. 53) past any 'last attempt', but W. P. Frith's painting *Ramsgate Sands* (1854) includes two young girls wearing Uglies.

Wide-brimmed round hats were also worn by women and children for riding (No. 26). By 1858 hats were accepted — except on formal occasions — and favoured by Queen Victoria and her ladies (No. 45). They were now made of silk, velvet, or plush (No. 56), often trimmed with a feather.

Hair was worn drawn off the face *à l'Imperatrice* — a style worn by the Empress Eugénie. The evening dress wreath of flowers was arranged at the back of the head, hanging down on the nape of the neck (Nos. 28, 51). From 1856 onward there were occasionally a few curls at the back. Side ringlets were seen no more on fashionable heads after 1852, though women with naturally curly hair could not bring themselves to give up this becoming style. The girl in No. 41 has a hair-style several years out of date.

Indoor caps were no longer essential. Even for the middle-aged a head dress of ribbons was regarded as adequate. Lewis Carroll photographed his aunts wearing such an arrangement (No. 34). The details of their dresses are quite up-to-date, but the loop of hair and curls, respectively, in front of the ears show how difficult it is for those no longer young to change their hair-style. The same applies to the ear-concealing cap of Mrs. Watson (No. 33). Baroness de Späth (Lady-in-Waiting to Queen Victoria's mother the Duchess of Kent) was too old to keep up in the race of fashion, though she has not altogether aban-doned the struggle, and sports a black wig (No. 23). Her appearance is typical of the 'forties, but the photograph was taken in 1852. The 'spaniel' loops of hair and the position of her wreath proclaim for No. 25 a date in the 'forties, but are contradicted by the extremely full flounces, which could hardly have

41

been achieved without considerable stiffening, and the quilling on the scarf — a detail of 1851. As one must go by the latest and not the earliest details, this daguerreotype may have been taken as late as 1851. So it is clear that human beings, apart from the ultra-fashionable, do not look like fashion-plates, even if they flatter themselves that they do. Incidentally, if it were obligatory to wear gloves indoors, all these ladies would have done so. The Princess Royal naturally wears white gloves with her confirmation dress of white silk with five vandyked flounces (No. 50). In those days French kid gloves fitting like a second skin so that the fingernails showed through were bought by the dozen for as little as 1s. to 1s. 6d. a pair. A still finer kind was sold packed in a walnut-shell. This was a revival of an eighteenth century fashion.

In 1850 skirts were less full than those of the previous year, but the difference can hardly be seen because they were covered with as many as five flounces, usually pinked and stamped at the edges. Even on morning dresses flounces were used more and more; three was the usual number. Instead of lying softly, as in the 'forties, they were stiffened to make them stick out. Often flounces were embroidered, or had a pattern of Bayadère stripes woven in the material (Nos. 39, 41, 43), or a narrow velvet border. Another idea in the mid-'fifties was to have many narrow flounces of thin material in two colours arranged alternately. The completion in 1855 of the new Balmoral Castle with its tartan interior decoration designed by Prince Albert gave great impetus to the spread of plaid and tartan patterns, not so much for curtains and carpets as for clothes (Nos. 34, 40, 44) and a variety of objects such as book-covers, purses, needle-cases, etc.

Unsuitably rich materials, usually patterned, were used for morning dresses. At French watering-places, 'Ladies walked by the sea in silk gowns, brocaded, or shot with gold and silver. One would have imagined oneself present at a ball at the Tuileries.'[1] At these resorts satin elastic-sided boots with 'high' heels were worn; elsewhere soft kid boots, often combined with patent leather; and indoors, heeled slippers.

In day dresses the rather high-necked bodice, with less steeply sloping shoulders than in the 'forties, often had a basque giving the effect of a jacket (Nos. 39, 41) or was in fact a jacket opening over a chemisette or (in 1851 and 1852) a masculine-style waistcoat—a fashion inevitably condemned as fast on its introduction. For the morning toilet chemisettes (like a blouse worn under the bodice, with collar and sleeves showing) or separate collars and under-sleeves of muslin or batiste were usually trimmed with *broderie anglaise* (Nos. 34, 39, 46). This embroidery was of Swiss, not English, origin and consisted in cutting

[1] Augustin Challamel, *The History of Fashion in France*, London, 1882.

out holes and sewing round them. The plain tight sleeve typical of the 'forties was replaced by pagoda sleeves (Nos. 34, 50, 56) — sleeves with elaborate puffs and frills (No. 46). Finally about 1857 the very wide sleeve was slit open and hung down in such a way that it was difficult to take up a glass of wine without dipping the sleeve in one's plate (Nos. 33, 39, 41, 43).

Fringe was the most fashionable trimming in 1856, especially on *bretelles* from the shoulder to the waist point. In May it was complained in Paris that 'bretelles are worn by half the little grisettes in the streets'. Obviously the time had come for them to be given up, but in England they were worn for a few seasons longer (Nos. 34, 39). In 1857 there was a craze for black lace (No. 51).

As the decade progressed, ball dresses became more and more overladen with ruches, *bouillons* (puffs), ribbons, flounces, and lace. The Empress Eugénie appeared at a ball in 1859 wearing a white satin dress trimmed with no fewer than 103 tulle flounces.[1] Women intending to dance always wore dresses of the gauziest description made of tulle or tarlatan — a kind of almost transparent muslin, often with gold stars or spots. The skirts were either covered with flounces, or consisted of multiple skirts caught up by bunches of artificial flowers (No. 30). The effect on arrival was of exquisite fairy-like daintiness, 'but before the end of a ball, they are crumpled and faded.' The low *décolletage* of these charming dresses deeply shocked a man from the provinces who exclaimed in disgust at a ball at the Tuileries in 1855, 'I haven't seen anything like that since I was weaned!'[2] Indeed, throughout most of the nineteenth century 'the high water mark of modesty would ebb after sunset some six inches'.[3]

As early as July 1853 some dressmakers inserted whalebone hoops into the lining of skirts to give 'the ample fan-like form which is so graceful and so rarely obtained'.[4] The following year *The Ladies' Companion* suggested putting pieces of straw underneath each flounce to stiffen it, with the comment: 'The hoops of our grandmothers cannot have been much wider than the skirts of the fashionable lady of the present day.'[5] Certainly there was a look of the 1740s and '50s about her clothes. Many were the devices for extending the skirt. They ranged from bands of plaited straw, through three or four rolls of crinoline (horsehair) material at the hem, and a revival of the Georgian whalebone hoop in the skirt lining, to the ingenious technique of rubber tubes inflated like the inner tubes of car tyres. A British patent of May 1856

[1] Max von Boehn, *Die Mode: Menschen und Moden im neunzehnten Jahrhundert*, Vol. III, 1843–1878, Munich, n.d. [1919].
[2] ibid.   [3] C. W. Cunnington, *English Women's Clothing in the Nineteenth Century*, 1937.
[4] *The Ladies' Companion*, 1853.   [5] ibid. 1854.

described a garment made of airtight material (not specified), 'with a small nozzle for the insertion of a bellows for inflating it, and a larger aperture for the escape of the air when the wearer wishes to sit down.' Presumably she had to carry the bellows about in order to re-inflate when she stood up again. Pneumatic tubes were the most favoured system in the mid-'fifties, yet at the same time many fashionable beauties still kept to the traditional method of distending their tulle or tarlatan ball dresses simply by an enormous number of starched and flounced muslin petticoats. 'Many belles now wear fourteen in evening dress. They go to a ball standing up in their carriages, and stand between the dances, for fear of crushing their dress and fourteen petticoats!'[1] Marshal Canrobert told a friend who asked his opinion of her dress that it reminded him of an object which he was very fond of. After some teazing, the French Commander-in-Chief revealed that the object in question was his tent in the Crimea. He said he thought it had come to life and followed him from Sebastopol to Paris.[2] In March 1855 Walburga von Hohenthal (later Lady Paget) saw for the first time in Berlin 'the lately invented monster, a very large crinoline'. This cannot yet have been one made of metal. When the young countess went to Windsor nearly three years later for the wedding of the Princess Royal to Prince Frederick William of Prussia, Queen Victoria requested the Prussian ladies not to wear their crinolines on account of lack of space in the Chapel Royal.[3] From this episode it is sometimes incorrectly inferred that the Queen abjured the crinoline. However, many photographs show her wearing one (No. 59), and 'The Fashionable Anthem' composed by *Punch*, with the refrain

> 'God Save our gracious Queen,
> Who won't wear crinoline'

should not be taken literally.

What do we mean by 'a crinoline'? The structurally supported skirt was not in itself a nineteenth-century invention, but appeared now for the third time in the history of European costume. Its predecessors were the farthingale of the late sixteenth and early seventeenth centuries (persisting throughout the seventeenth century at the Spanish Court) and the eighteenth-century whalebone hoop-petticoat which disappeared from everyday use before the French Revolution, though it remained obligatory at the English Court until the

---

[1] *The Ladies' Companion*, April 1856.
[2] Anon. *Crinoline und Amazonenhut*, 2nd edition, Nordhausen, 1858.
[3] Walburga, Lady Paget. *Embassies of Other Days*, Vol. I, 1923.

accession of George IV in 1820. Stiffened petticoats and pneumatic tubes hardly come under the definition of a crinoline. The name abandoned all connection with horsehair and was applied to a separate cage of steel springs in hoops of increasing diameter to the bottom, connected with tapes or curved steel ribs. Sometimes it was incorporated in a petticoat, forming a contraption rather in the form of a gigantic old-fashioned lampshade. The crinoline not only expanded the skirt to enormous dimensions; it gave a different outline from the stuffed tea-cosy or bell shape produced by many petticoats. 'All the robes continue to be spread out like fans' reported a fashion journalist from Paris. 'Observe I say fans, *not* bells : the bell-shaped robe is now absurd.'[1]

A characteristic feature of the crinoline was not only its amplitude at the bottom, which preserved its wearer from the absurdity of looking like a bell, but the graceful swinging with which it reacted to every movement of its occupant. When she sat down, it tilted up in front, when she stood close to a table, it tilted up behind, when she walked, it swayed from side to side. Women's ankles, invisible for twenty years, were now revealed in tantalizing glimpses. Fancy coloured stockings naturally followed soon.

Punch, always quick to make fun of the latest fashions, referred to the *jupon squelette* in June 1856 and first illustrated a cage crinoline in August. Before that, the wide-skirt jokes concerned pneumatic tubes. These were not immediately discarded, for in January 1857 there is a cartoon of two girls inflating their air-tubes.

The introduction of the metal crinoline in the summer of 1856 was welcomed by most women with relief. It was indeed a great technical improvement, fulfilling the desire for wide skirts without impeding the legs by hot and heavy petticoats, and giving by contrast with its size an illusion of slenderness to the waist without the need for tight-lacing. The inventor of the cage, a Frenchman (unnamed) is said to have made 250,000 francs (£10,000) in five weeks.[2] I believe the inventor to be R. C. Milliet of Besançon, whose agent in Britain, C. Amet, was granted the first British patent for a metal crinoline in July 1856[3] — a 'skeleton petticoat made of steel springs fastened to tape'. The patent was, of course, applied for in January, and the crinoline probably went into production under provisional protection. Milliet's patent for 'une tournure de femme' (classified under haberdashery) dated 24 April 1856, specifies 'elastic extensible circles joined together by vertical bands'. 'Elastic' is here used in its narrow sense of springy, flexible. Had the agent Amet

[1] *The Ladies' Companion*, August 1857.
[2] Anon. *Crinoline und Amazonenhut*, 2nd edition, Nordhausen, 1858.
[3] British patent No. 1729, 22 July 1856.

specified 'vertical bands' instead of 'tape', the British patent would have covered more constructions of crinoline, and made still more money for the inventor on the English market. The largest firm of crinoline manufacturers was Thomson, whose London factory, employing over a thousand women, produced up to 4000 crinolines daily. Another branch of this firm, in Saxony, produced over 9½ million crinolines in the course of a dozen years.[1]

Nearly all men heartily disliked the crinoline until they got used to it, and in Germany many swore they would not marry a girl who wore one. The cage was considered to make women unapproachable — though the manufacturers of the 'Sansflectum' claimed that it would 'bear a good squeeze without getting out of order'. Unless great care were taken, ordinary crinolines tilted up and revealed too much. 'The other day we observed Mrs. Paragon and her two daughters walking in Regent-street. The young ladies were walking close to, and one on each side of their mother. Consequently their respective crinolines were tilted up in the air on the "off-side". An opportunity was thus afforded to all anxious spectators to study the manufacture of the young ladies' balmorals [boots], and the fit of their open-worked silk stockings over their ankles, a word which is now by courtesy applied to some eighteen inches or thereabouts of the leg.'[2] To avoid such 'shocking' sights Edward Philpott, a draper in Piccadilly, brought out 'The patent Ondina or Waved Jupon [costing 18s. 6d.–26s. 6d. according to the quality of the cover material] [which] does away with the unsightly results of the ordinary hoops; and so perfect are the wave-like bands, that a lady may ascend a steep stair, lean against a table, throw herself into an armchair, pass to her stall at the Opera, or occupy a fourth seat in a carriage, without inconvenience to herself or others, or provoking the rude remarks of the observers, thus modifying, in an important degree, all those peculiarities tending to destroy the modesty of Englishwomen; and lastly, it allows the dress to fall into graceful folds'.[3]

Anxiety about the crushing of skirts was at an end, but fresh difficulties arose as the crinoline, by the inevitable process of emulation, grew ever larger. The cares of the hostess were increased by the expanded garments of her visitors dressed in the height, or rather breadth, of fashion. Where before two or three women had sat on a sofa, there was now barely room for the skirts of one. An unwary movement might upset an occasional-table laden with *bric-à-brac*, or even the wearer herself, with embarrassing consequences. The Duchess

[1] W. Born, 'Crinoline and Bustle', *CIBA Review*, No. 46, 1943.
[2] 'Crinoline', an anonymous article reprinted from *The Illustrated News of the World*, London, n.d. (1863).
[3] Edward Philpott, *Crinoline in our Parks and Promenades from 1710 to 1864*, London, n.d. (1864).

of Manchester, who looks so dignified in evening dress (No. 61), caught her hoops in climbing over a stile and landed upside down, exhibiting a pair of scarlet knickers (then still a new-fangled garment) to the startled gaze of the Duc de Malakoff, who declared, 'c'était diabolique!' Quite apart from such mishaps, the sheer size alone of the crinoline was an inconvenience, and provided a favourite theme for cartoonists. Everybody made fun of it, and it was said that the omnibus companies were going to make a new regulation obliging passengers to take off their cages before entering and hang them up outside the vehicle! Plain old maids, servants, and poor people — always a butt for Victorian humour — are invariably depicted in contemporary drawings and in *Punch* with clumsy hoops showing through too-scanty petticoats.

Joking apart, the crinoline was a decidedly dangerous contraption. Occasionally the hoops of pedestrians got entangled in carriage wheels, and in windy weather the wearers risked being blown off their feet, or even over a cliff. With luck, the crinoline might act as a parachute. The most frequent, and often fatal, accidents were caused by fire, for it was impossible to save the victim by rolling her in a rug. The light fabrics worn in the evening were a contributory factor, tulle and muslin being the most inflammable of textiles. The worst catastrophe occurred on 8 December 1863 when 2000 women were burnt to death in the Cathedral at Santiago, Chile, because the vast quantities of inflammable material in their dresses fed the flames.[1] 'Take what precautions we may against fire, so long as the hoop is worn, life is never safe. All are living under a sentence of death which may occur unexpectedly in the most appalling form.'[2] *Punch* proposed that ladies should wear their 'birdcages' *outside* the dress as a fireguard, or that the pneumatic tubes which continued to be used by some, should be filled with water. But the possible danger of burning to death seemed more remote than the embarrassing probability of springing a leak.

Social reformers objected that the wearing of crinolines encouraged concealment of pregnancy, and consequently, infanticide.

The crinoline reached its apogee in 1859–64 (Nos. 57, 58, 60, 61, 62, 67, 68, 69, 70). In 1859–60, so the art and social historian Max von Boehn claimed, dresses measured ten yards round the hem.[3] Sceptical of this dimension, which has been repeated by other experts, I made a ten yard circle of string on the floor, which once and for all settled the matter in a practical demonstration.

[1] Max von Boehn, *Die Mode: Menschen und Moden im neunzehnten Jahrhundert*, Vol. III, 1843–1878, Munich, n.d. [1919].

[2] 'Crinoline', an anonymous article reprinted from *The Illustrated News of the World*, London, n.d. (1863).

[3] Max von Boehn, *Die Mode: Menschen und Moden im neunzehnten Jahrhundert*, Vol. III, 1843–1878, Munich, n.d. [1919].

Judging from this, in conjunction with photographs — not fashion drawings — the bottom hoop of even the largest crinoline was not more than $5\frac{1}{2}$ to 6 yards in circumference. The full skirt falling in loose folds over it would have a larger circumference, but in no case could it possibly have approached ten yards. Counting flounces and other trimmings, the quantity of material used was vast. An evening dress of 1859 with four skirts, each trimmed with ruches, required 1,100 yards of tulle.[1]

Queen Victoria's eldest child (later the Empress Frederick) appears in the full panoply of crinoline with two flounces of magnificent lace (No. 57). The Empress Eugénie wears a comparatively plain day dress of silk trimmed with bold applications of broad pleating (No. 58). The Empress was conservative in her taste and no innovator of fashions, according to her *couturier* Charles Frederick Worth.

In 1858 re-appeared the Princess dress in which bodice and skirt were made without a join at the waist, the fullness of the skirt being achieved by shaped gores. There were also some dresses made with a round waist finished with a belt or sash, but this type was slow to catch on. The pointed bodices which women had been accustomed to for over twenty years were still preferred to the new round and slightly higher waistline, for 'a round waist with the addition of a bouffante skirt renders a woman very like a tun'. As the round waistline established itself in the early 'sixties, the ungraceful effect was overcome by reducing the diameter of the top hoop, and goring the skirt so that it did not jut out suddenly at the top. The crinoline remained enormously wide at the bottom, but the steel hoops — up to thirty-five in number — instead of being circular were slightly flattened in front. By 1864 every effort was made to cause the figure to appear slim just below the waist. The more effectually the breadths of the material were gored and the fewer pleats required around the waist, the more fashionable was the dress considered. The skirt increased gradually in width to the hem, and in the mid- and late-'sixties it had a straight instead of a curved outline (Nos. 83, 84, 85, 90). The dome had turned into a funnel (whereas in the eighteenth century, the funnel shape had turned into a dome).

Wide flounces were found to give an overladen appearance over a large crinoline, but rows of narrow flounces were still sometimes to be seen, especially in thin materials (Nos. 61, 62). Trimming in the early 'sixties was often confined to the lower part of the skirt, which was ornamented in a variety of ways: two or three narrow fluted flounces often arranged asymmetrically,

---

[1] Max von Boehn, *Die Mode: Menschen und Moden im neunzehnten Jahrhundert*, Vol. III, 1843-1878, Munich, n.d. [1919].

62 *Princess Mary of Cambridge (later Duchess of Teck), by Camille Silvy, London, c. 1861*

61 *The Duchess of Manchester, by Camille Silvy, London c. 1863*

63　Group at a country house, by H. W. Verschoyle, c. 1862

64 *Group on the terrace of a country house, by Charles Nègre, c. 1863 (Lord Brougham with family and friends at Cannes)*

66   *The Prince of Wales, by J. E. Mayall, March 1863*

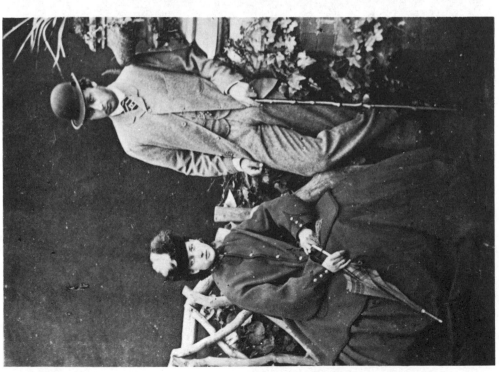

65   *The Prince and Princess of Wales at Sandringham, autumn 1863*

67   *Mrs. James Bœch, c. 1863*

68   *The Duchess of Sutherland, by Disdéri, Paris,*
c. 1864

70 *The crinoline, c. 1864*

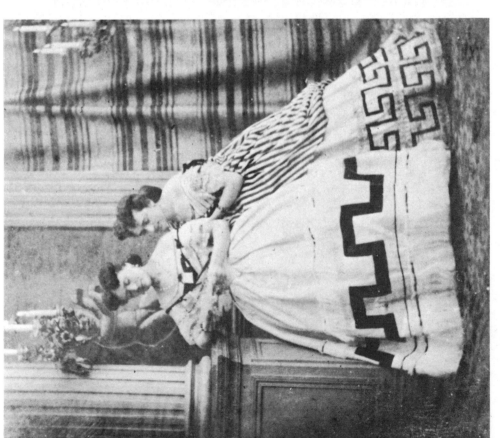

69 *Two evening dresses, c. 1864*

71 *Princess Alice of Hesse and one of her daughters,*
    photographed at Balmoral by G. W. Wilson, c. 1866

72 *Winter walking dress, c. 1863*

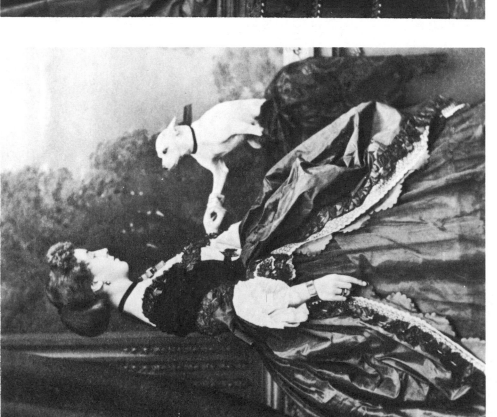

73 *Lady Diana Beauclerk, by F. R. Window, London, c. 1866*

74 *The Princess of Solmes, Comtesse Ratazzi, in evening dress, by Disdéri, Paris, c. 1867*

76   *Dr. Mary Walker, c.* 1865

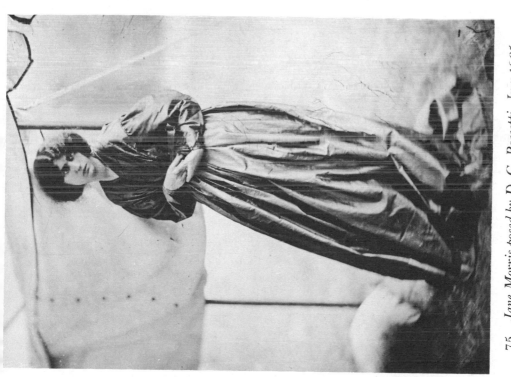

75   *Jane Morris posed by D. G. Rossetti, July* 1865

78 *Lady's riding-habit, mid-sixties*

77 *Country suit, c. 1867*

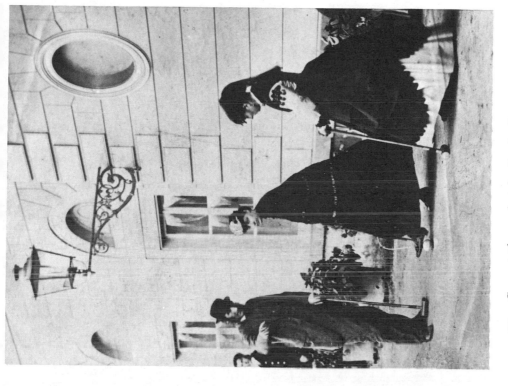

80 *Croquet players in 'short' crinolines, c. 1866*

79 **Woman alpinist in crinoline on the Grindelwald glacier, by Adolphe Braun, c. 1863**

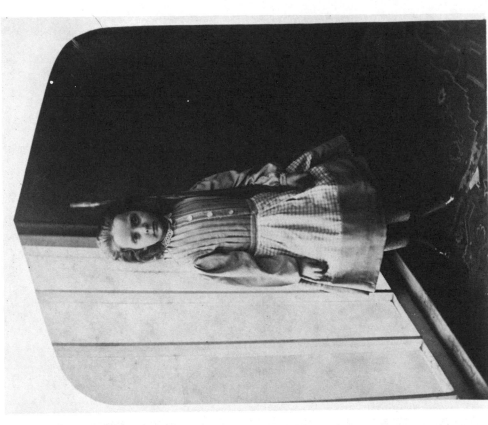

82 *Ella Monier Williams, by Lewis Carroll, 1866*

81 *A girl, by Ghémar frères, Brussels, c. 1862*

84   *The Princess of Wales, by Disdéri, c. 1866*

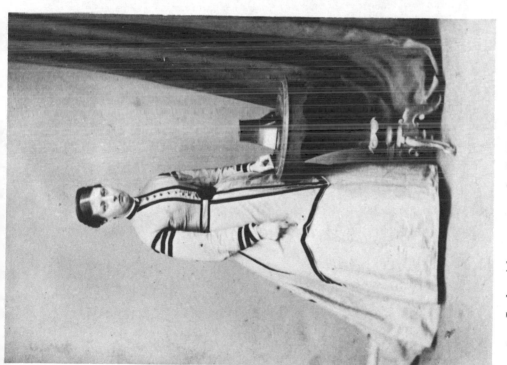

83   *Lady with stereoscope, by J. Harsnurzh, c. 1867*

85 *A group
in the country,*

86   *Archery group, c. 1868*

87   *A family at Wimbledon, c. 1869*

88 *The Empress Elisabeth of Austria
by Rabending. Vienna, c. 1869*

89 *Lady, by Jabez Hughes, Ryde, I.o.W. c. 1869*

90 *Mary Helen Ferguson, by I. Wood, Aberdeen,*
c. 1868

91 *Simple house dress, by F. Gutekunst, Philadelphia, c. 1870*

93   *A lady, by Maull & Co., London, c. 1869*

92   *The Hon. Mrs. George Pennant (later Baroness Penrhyn), c. 1868*

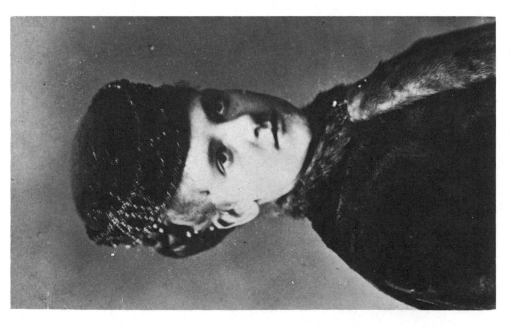

94   *A casquette, c. 1869, by Elliott & Fry, London*

95   *A 'lamballe plateau', c. 1869, by Icilio Calzolari, Milan*

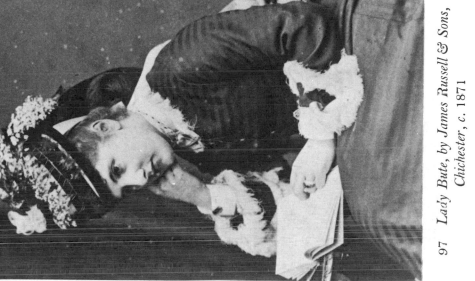

97 *Lady Bute, by James Russell & Sons,*
Chichester, c. 1871

96 *Elaborate hair style of 1868–9, by the London*
Stereoscopic Co.

99 *A lady, by C. S. Cork, Hadleigh, c. 1870*

98 *Outdoor dress and matching jacket, c. 1870*

101 *Prince Leopold and Princess Louise, 1870*

100 *The Comtesse de Pourtalès, by Le Jeune, Paris, 1870*

103 *A lady, by G. W. Wilson, Aberdeen, c. 1872*

102 *A lady, by G. W. Wilson, Aberdeen, c. 1874*

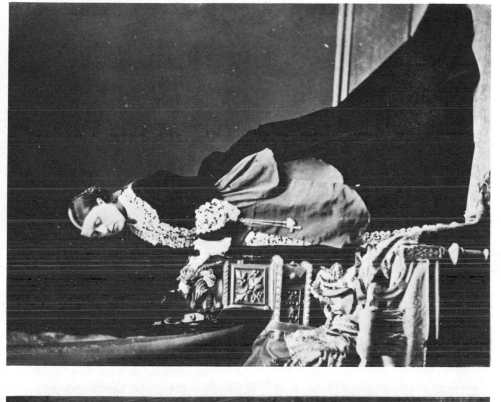

105   *The Hon. L. Kerr, c. 1873*

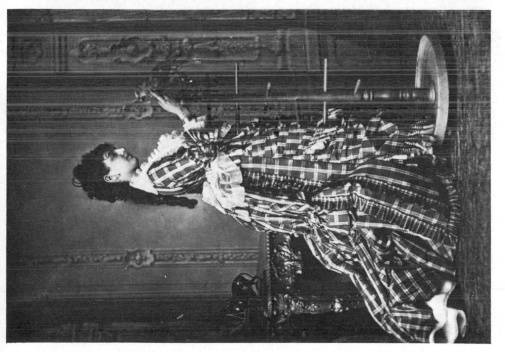

104   *A lady with parrot, by Liébert, Paris c. 1375*

107 *A lady, c. 1875*

106 *Mrs. T. R. T. Hodgson, c. 1872*

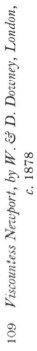

109 *Viscountess Newport, by W. & D. Downey, London,*
c. 1878

108 *Mrs. Rousby in yachting dress and 'boater',*
c. 1870

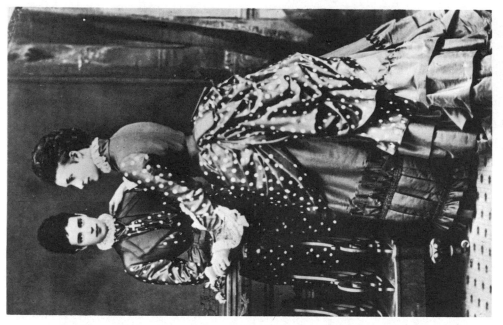

111　The Princess of Wales (right) and her sister
Dagmar, later the Czarina, during the latter's visit
to London in 1873

110　A lady, by R. F. Barnes, c. 1876

113 *The Princess of Wales, by Horatio Nelson King.*
    London, c. 1874

112 *The Prince of Wales, c. 1875*

115 *The Prince of Wales, by W. & D. Downey,*
October 1876

114 *Shooting outfits, early seventies*

117 *Tricycling costume, by Benda: Prague, 1878–9*

116 *Tennis in tied-back skirts and trains, c. 1873*

118   *Resting after tennis, c. 1875*

119   *Daughters of the Duke of Buckingham,*
Governor General of Madras, c. 1877

rows of pleating, or velvet applied in bands (No. 55) or geometrical patterns such as vandykes and the Greek meander pattern (No. 69). In 1864–66 a popular trimming was to have different coloured or black straps down each seam of the gored skirt. Materials were on the whole heavier than in the 'fifties and frequently plain. *Moiré antique* (watered silk) was extensively used (No. 84).

Broad sashes were often worn with the round-waisted dresses, and in Paris young girls tied them at the back, matrons in front. The bodices of ball dresses, if no sash were worn, were still slightly pointed and often had berthas or drapery *à la grecque:* formal full dress has a tendency towards conservatism.

In the early 'sixties Bishop sleeves were more frequent than the wide pagoda or bell sleeves, which were still worn, alongside new variations (No. 60). *Broderie anglaise* on *engageantes* had become too common and dropped quite out of favour.

Zouave jackets on the lines of a sleeved bolero, and blouse-like Garibaldi chemisettes introduced in a wave of admiration following Garibaldi's invasion of Sicily in 1860 soon became general for casual wear (No. 55, centre). In 1862 it was decreed: 'For morning and boudoir toilets the bodice to the dress is quite exploded; instead of it, a very long skirt is worn, with a Garibaldi chemisette.'[1] Little girls' dresses also had a loose bodice (Nos. 81, 82), their pantalettes no longer showed, and often their hair was uncurled and simply combed back in Alice in Wonderland style. Lewis Carroll, whose chief hobby between 1856 and 1880 was photography, portrayed his numerous young friends in their crinoline frocks (No. 82). Boys wore knickerbockers and a waist-length loose jacket.

Out of doors women presented in the years 1861–64 a triangular tent-like outline, the waist being concealed by a long loose cloak or mantle, and the 'spoon' bonnet with upward-pointing brim forming the apex of the pyramid (No. 67).

The spoon bonnet was not officially buried by *Punch* until the end of 1864, but the 'Bibi' which ousted it had been introduced in the spring. The Bibi was so small that it looked almost like a cap. The first woman to venture out in a bonnet without a *bavolet* was Madame Worth. Her husband's first important customer, Princess Metternich — always in the advance guard of fashion — considered the curtainless bonnet charming, but everyone else was shocked because it revealed the back of the neck (for the first time in well over twenty years). 'I never saw anything so perfectly disgusting' objected a prude. 'That hat is simply indecent.'[2] Which only proves how relative decency is, for

[1] *The Queen*, 1862.   [2] Jean Philippe Worth, *A Century of Fashion*, Boston, 1928.

exceedingly low-necked evening dresses were in fashion. In 1865 a still tinier bonnet was invented, the 'fanchon' composed often nearly entirely of flowers.

As the 'sixties progressed hats became more widely worn, yet however elaborately trimmed with flowers, fringe, beads, or humming birds, a hat was always less formal than a bonnet.

'It is long enough since a bonnet meant shelter to the face or protection to the head' protested Mrs. Lynn Linton. 'That fragment of a bonnet which at present represents the head gear is now poised on the front, and ornamented with birds, portions of beasts, reptiles, and insects. We have seen a bonnet composed of a rose and a couple of feathers, another of two or three butterflies or as many beads and a bit of lace, and a third represented by five green leaves joined at the stalks.'[1]

Since 1864 hats and bonnets had left the back of the head free to allow room for the large chignon of hair, often of a Titian reddish-yellow colour. In the early 'sixties the hair was often simply bundled into a chenille hairnet at the back, but later it was arranged more elaborately (Nos. 70, 96). In Paris fragile exotic butterflies worth £4 or £5 each[2] and real humming-birds[3] were worn in the hair with ball dress. 'The fashion of wearing the hair is every day growing more exaggerated. At the back of the head, chignons, bows and curls are placed *en masse*, descending a considerable way down the nape of the neck. Scarcely an attempt is made of hiding the quantity of artificial hair with which every female head is encumbered, to the great benefit of coiffeurs and *artistes en cheveux* in general.'[4] Curls on the forehead, instead of a simple centre-parting, began to reappear in the mid-'sixties after a lapse of over forty years (No. 73). In the late 'sixties the chignon climbed up the back of the head until a fashionable hat or bonnet was perched on the forehead (Nos. 94, 95). The Lamballe *plateau* of 1866–69 (No. 95), round or oval, was named after Marie Antoinette's friend, the Princesse de Lamballe.

Winter mantles in the first half of the 'sixties were often trimmed with military braiding and astrakhan (No. 68).

Summer 1864 saw the beginning of the short loose *sac paletot* and *casaque* of the same material as the dress (No. 85 centre) amounting to a two-piece suit. They had the rather narrow fitted masculine coat sleeve which came into fashion the previous year.

As early as 1857 women looped up their skirts, revealing the petticoat, as a temporary measure in the country or on the beach — not in town (Nos. 45, 52). In 1859 Princess Pauline von Metternich, wife of the Austrian Ambas-

---

[1] *The Saturday Review*, London, July 1867.   [3] ibid. 1866.
[2] *The Queen*, 1863.   [4] ibid. 1864.

sador in Paris, visited the Empress Eugénie at Fontainebleau wearing a skirt looped up to display a fancy petticoat. 'Le singe à la mode' as the chic but plain princess called herself, was much admired for her taste in dress, and after this the practice of drawing up the skirt in festoons by means of an arrangement of cords and rings inside it, became fairly general in Paris when out of doors.[1] In England, women still allowed their dresses to trail on the ground in town, but in the country (Nos. 71, 72) and for archery (No. 86), croquet (No. 80) and similar activities, the looped-up dress was worn from 1860 onward. The petticoat of scarlet flannel, taffeta or alpaca in some other bright colour such as magenta, was often trimmed at the edge with bands of contrasting material (No. 72). Frequently coloured stockings with horizontal black stripes matched the petticoat. The drawn-up skirt was called the Pompadour style, although the Marquise died ten years before the similar fashion in the 1770s and '80s. Coloured petticoats were informal and could only be worn with walking dress; 'the petticoat for a *toilette habillée* should always be white under all circumstances', and so were the stockings.

From now on a distinction was made between walking dress and visiting dress, which remained as long as ever. Before the mid-'sixties comparatively few fashion plates illustrate 'short' dresses. Reversing the normal progress of women's fashions, what started as a practical measure eventually became acceptable in society. Although not its initiator, the Empress Eugénie played a part in the acceptance of this mode. The Empress and her ladies adopted walking dresses of barely ankle length just reaching to the tops of their high-heeled boots when accompanying the Imperial stag-hunt at Compiègne in the autumn. The extravagance of the Court was so great that only very rich people could accept an invitation to Compiègne without anxiety. It was known that the Emperor and Empress did not like to see anyone wearing the same dress twice, and no fewer than twenty eight separate toilets were required for a week's stay — four changes a day.[2] The prestige attached to such extravagance was enough to popularize any fashion — even a practical one! In a short dress of this kind Eugénie once went for a drive at Salzburg with the Emperor and Empress of Austria — the beautiful Elisabeth wearing a conventional long gown. 'Take care how you get into the carriage, my dear,' Franz Joseph warned his wife, with a pointed glance at Eugénie's legs, 'or someone might catch sight of your feet.'[3]

The Empress Eugénie, wishing to send the Queen of Madagascar a present

---

[1] *The Queen*, 1862.   [2] ibid.
[3] Max von Boehn, *Die Mode: Menschen und Moden im neunzehnten Jahrhundert*, Vol. III, 1843–1878, Munich, n.d. [1919].

on the occasion of her proclamation as sovereign in May 1863, enquired what she would like to have. The reply was, a fashionable Paris dress. The Empress ordered Worth to make two gold- and silver-embroidered velvet dresses, one scarlet, the other green, with crinolines to match. When Queen Rasoherina sent for the French Ambassador to convey her thanks to the Empress, he could hardly keep a straight face. The Queen sat with the red velvet gown trailing for yards all around her, and the red cashmere crinoline hanging above her as a State canopy.[1]

By 1866 it began to be felt that a long dress which could be adapted to serve for both walking and visiting in a carriage savoured too much of economy, and in the newest walking dresses the skirt was not drawn up, but actually made shorter than the matching petticoat, which was often not a separate garment, but simulated in the form of a band trimmed with two rows of black velvet ribbon. In this type of dress the skirt was so much gored that it stretched tightly over the framework of the crinoline like a lampshade. The hem was cut out in scallops, vandykes, or turrets. The cage, though now diminished in size, was still obligatory, for 'only very eccentric ladies, and those who desire to be conspicuous, are seen totally without crinoline out of doors'.[2] It was certainly not the wish to be conspicuous that caused Florence Nightingale to abjure the crinoline, and aesthetic rather than eccentric is the adjective applicable to the Pre-Raphaelite beauty Mrs. William Morris (No. 75). Desire for emancipation was the motive for the rational dress of the American Dr. Mary Walker (No. 76) — a dress which, incidentally, is quite different from the costume designed some fifteen years earlier by her compatriot Mrs. Amelia Bloomer.

To fashion journalists in 1866 it seemed, in contrast to the vast ballooning skirts of a few seasons previously, that 'skirts are now cut as scantily, and are as devoid of pleats, as during the first Napoleon's reign'.[3] The adjustable long dress which could be looped up continued to be worn for at least another year. There were also dresses made with a looped-up skirt over a trained petticoat or underskirt — a travesty of the whole principle of the looped-up skirt intended to facilitate walking. Two crinolines were needed; a short and fairly narrow cone-shaped one for walking dress, giving a bottle-shaped outline, and a larger one for the evening, projecting at the back to support the train. The round waist was higher than before, and 'the crinoline alone preserves us from the ungraceful style of dress in vogue under the First French Empire, the scant gored skirts and short waists'.[4]

Already at the end of 1865 progressive young women smoking cigarettes

[1] Jean Philippe Worth, *A Century of Fashion*, 1928.
[2] *The Queen*, 1866.   [3] ibid. 1866.   [4] *The Englishwoman's Domestic Magazine*, 1865.

were depicted by George Du Maurier in trained indoor dresses with no crinolines. The following July *Punch* shows ladies reprimanding their servant for *leaving off* her crinoline. Four years earlier, the same journal had illustrated a maid being ordered to take off her crinoline because she looked ridiculous: by the late 'sixties it was distinguished and rather daring *not* to wear a crinoline at all indoors (No. 88, 89) — and the maid seemed to be competing with her mistress.

The straighter, narrower skirts of 1866 were frequently trimmed with narrow bands of black velvet simulating an overskirt. Peplums were worn, often with the four points ending in tassels. 'No dressy afternoon toilet is considered complete without a peplum. Up to this month [April] peplums were only worn with ball dresses, but now they are to be seen in the Bois and other fashionable promenades.'[1] The peplum (No. 83) remained in fashion until 1868. Bodices had high round waists, a square neckline filled in with a chemisette of tucked muslin, and long tight sleeves. The evening *décolletage* was as low as ever, and without a bertha. Long Empire-style gloves were worn.

After so many years of voluminous petticoats and crinolines the narrower skirts seemed very strange. 'It is scarcely credible to what eccentricities the very flat scant skirts are leading. There is neither pleat nor wrinkle in the upper part of the skirt; it is in fact an exact copy of the style worn during the First Empire. . . . Crinoline has not entirely disappeared but it is now reduced to three circles of steel at the lower part of the skirt, and these circles measure from $2\frac{1}{2}$ to $2\frac{3}{4}$ yards in circumference.'[2] This was, however, not a fact but a forecast, and not only the truthful photograph but also the Paris fashion-plates continue to show large crinolines alongside a very small proportion of 'Empire' dresses.

With the trained Empire-style dress a bonnet was imperative, for a bonnet was more formal than a hat, which was worn with the short walking dress. Bonnets were often tied at the back with narrow strings under the chignon, and were then difficult to distinguish from a small hat. A *casquette* was like an old-fashioned telegraph boy's or hotel page boy's cap, worn tipped forward (No. 94). The shape was the same as Garibaldi's cap.

Provincial women who had been against the crinoline on its introduction had meanwhile become used to it and wanted to keep it. While the crinoline dwindled away in the cities, it was noticed by a feudal type of landowner in the wilds of Wales who gave 'wholesale notice to quit to her tenants in Carmarthenshire and Pembrokeshire, in consequence of their wives and daughters wearing crinoline, a practice to which Miss Lloyd of Laques objects'.[3]

[1] *The Queen*, 1866.   [2] ibid. 1867.   [3] *The Oswestry Advertiser*, 1867.

The Rise and Fall of the Crinoline

At the height of its popularity the crinoline permeated all classes and was regarded as indispensable for everything except riding (No. 78). It was worn not only by fashionable women but by their maids, by peasant girls in the fields, by factory workers, by mountaineers (No. 79), on the beach (No. 52), by actresses in historical plays. In Weimar Christine Hebbel-Enghaus played Kriemhild in Hebbel's *Nibelungen* wearing this most unsuitable attire for a tragedy of the Dark Ages. Her death scene turned the tragedy almost into a French farce. Lying on the stage with her feet towards the auditorium, Kriemhild's crinoline ballooned up and offered the spectators a splendid view of her underclothes![1] In Paris, too, frightful anachronisms appeared in the serious as well as in the light theatre: Mlle Clairon played Medea, and Hortense Schneider Helen of Troy in Offenbach's *La Belle Hélène*, in crinolines. At a fancy-dress ball given at the French Foreign Office by Madame Walewska, crinolines were worn by guests dressed in medieval robes, as Olympian goddesses, and even as angels.[2]

It was during the crinoline period that chemical dyes began replacing vegetable dyes — though as late as 1900 a woad factory still survived near Wisbech. The first of the aniline dyes, a brilliant purple, was discovered by chance in 1856 by William Henry Perkin, an industrial chemist of eighteen, in the course of experiments on the production of synthetic quinine from the waste products of coal-gas undertakings. In the 'sixties purple, mauve, and the bright purplish-pink or fuchsia shades named Magenta and Solferino in honour of Napoleon III's victories over the Austrians in 1859, were all the rage. Another chemical dye was a vivid emerald green containing arsenite of copper. This was abandoned by Parisians in the early 'sixties following a report in the *Union Médicale* of the illness of a young woman who went to a ball in a green dress and was poisoned.[3] A Berlin physician testified that no less than 60 grains of arsenic powdered off from a single dress in the course of an evening's dancing — enough to kill thirty people if administered in doses.[4] In London an artificial-flower maker succumbed to the effects of working on wreaths coloured with this arsenical dye (which, incidentally, was used for the bright green cloth covers of many Victorian books). The danger was soon forgotten, however, and emerald green as well as brilliant purples and pinks, and 'azuline' blue of a garishness never seen today, were the most popular shades. Such colours needed to be used with discretion, and combined with black or neutral

---

[1] Max von Boehn, *Die Mode: Menschen und Moden im neunzehnten Jahrhundert*, Vol. III, Munich, n.d. [1919].

[2] Henri Bouchot, *Les Elégances du Second Empire*, Paris, n.d. (1897).

[3] Augustin Challamel, *The History of Fashion in France*, London, 1882.

[4] *The Queen*, 1861.

tints. Unfortunately Englishwomen tended to lack colour sense and a knowledge of what suited them. Even in the days of the softer vegetable dyes, they were rebuked by Mrs. Merrifield for wearing bright colours 'without reference to their accordance with the complexion of the wearer. We continually see a light blue bonnet and flowers surrounding a sallow countenance, or a pink opposed to one of a glowing red; a pale complexion associated with canary or lemon yellow, or one of delicate red and white rendered almost colourless by the vicinity of deep red. It must be confessed that we English have always been more remarkable for our partiality to gay or glaring colours, than for our skill in adapting them to the person, or arranging them so as to be in harmony with each other. . . . Let us note the colours on the dresses of the first six ladies we meet. What do we see first? A fancy straw bonnet, lined and trimmed with rose colour, an orange shawl, and a lilac muslin dress. The next wears a blue bonnet, lilac *visite*, and a pink dress. A third has a violet bonnet, pink bows outside, sky-blue strings, and a green veil!' and so on.[1]

The French philosopher and art historian Hippolyte Taine had a similarly uncomplimentary opinion of Englishwomen's taste in the 'sixties. 'Their dress, loud and overcharged with ornament, is that of a woman of easy virtue, or a *parvenue*. One is always startled at the spectacle of this paraphernalia draped on an obviously respectable young woman. On Sundays in Hyde Park such sartorial excesses on the persons of ladies and girls belonging to the rich middle-class are very shocking. . . . Beauty and adornment are abundant, but there is a want of taste. The colours are outrageously crude, and lines ungraceful. Crinolines too full, or the fullness badly draped, like geometrical cones or cloc dented; ribbons and scarves, green; gold lacing; bold, flower-patterned materials; a profusion of floating gauze; hair bunched, falling or curled. The whole display surmounted by tiny hats, much trimmed but hardly perceptible. The hats are over trimmed, the hair too shiny and clamped to the temples with too hard a line; the *mantelet* or *casaque* hangs shapeless to the hips, the skirt is monstrously overfull, and the whole of this scaffolding is badly put together, badly matched, striped, fussed, overdone, loud, excessively numerous colours each swearing at the others. . . . One sees purple or poppy-red silks, grass-green dresses decorated with flowers, azure blue scarves.'[2] It was, of course, the ostentatious newly-rich business people who merited Taine's criticism. People of higher standing often had a taste for simpler clothes.

Influenced probably by the extravagance and artificiality of the Second Empire, a more sophisticated type of girl appeared in the late 'sixties than

[1] Mary Philadelphia Merrifield, *Dress as a Fine Art*, London, 1854.
[2] *Taine's Notes on England*, translated by Edward Hyams, 1957.

any during the previous thirty years. 'High' heels (at the most $1\frac{1}{2}''$), 'short' skirts (ending just above the ankle), chignons of extra hair, make-up, and other adjuncts to beauty, were abominated by the admirers of the gentle, drooping womanhood of the 'forties and 'fifties.

Eliza Lynn Linton, a journalist and novelist of forty-five who separated from her husband in 1867, castigated modern girls as well as modern fashions in *The Saturday Review* on several occasions during this and the following year. Even allowing for the critical attitude towards the young commonly manifested by the older generation, Mrs. Lynn Linton's attack is so vituperative that one cannot overcome the suspicion that her husband had been lured away by the artificial charms of 'the girl of the period . . . a creature who dyes her hair and paints her face'.[1] 'The apparent object of modern female dress', declared Mrs. Linton, 'is to assimilate its wearers as quickly as possible in appearance to women of a certain class. There are pearl-powder, violet-powder, rouge, bistre for the eyelids, bella donna for the eyes, whitelead and blacklead, yellow dye and mineral acids for the hair. When fashionable Madame has painted and varnished her face, she then proceeds, like Jesebel, to tire her head, and whether she has much hair or little, she fixes on the back of it a huge nest of coarse hair generally well baked in order to free it from the parasites with which it abounded when it first adorned the person of some Russian or North German peasant girl.'[2] With understandable indignation the writer castigates the falsehood of certain fashionable aids to improve the wearer's appearance. 'Some of these votaries of dress find their ears too long, or too large, or ill placed, but a prettier or better shaped pair are easily purchased, admirably moulded in guttapercha or some other plastic material; they are delicately coloured, fitted up with earrings and a spring apparatus, and they are then adjusted on to the head, the despised natural ears being, of course, carefully hidden from view.' 'Falsies' are by no means an invention of our time but were well known to mid-Victorian women. A French firm advertised '*poitrines adhérentes* of pink rubber, which follow the movements of respiration with mathematical and perfect precision'.[3] More objectionable was the *demi-temps*, an anterior bustle worn ostensibly to make the folds of the dress fall properly, but in reality — so Mrs. Lynn Linton claimed — to give the appearance of advanced pregnancy. Had this trick worked with William Linton, one wonders? 'Thus it comes to be a grave matter of doubt, when a man marries, how

---

[1] Essay on 'The Girl of the Period' (unsigned, by Mrs. Lynn Linton) in *The Saturday Review*, London, 14 March 1868.

[2] Essay on 'Costume and its Morals' (unsigned, by Mrs. Lynn Linton) in *The Saturday Review*, London, 13 July 1867.

[3] ibid. 13 July 1867.

much is real of the woman who has become his wife. Her bones, her debts, and her caprices may be the only realities which she can bestow on her husband. All the rest — hair, teeth, complexion, ears, bosom, figure, including the *demi-temps* — are alike an imposition and a falsehood.'[1] By using such devices the girl of the period 'whose sole idea of life is plenty of fun and luxury' defeated her own object — to find a rich husband — and only succeeded in making men afraid of her, 'with her false red hair and painted skin, talking slang as glibly as a man, and by preference leading the conversation to doubtful subjects.'[2]

In 1868–69 it was touch and go whether straight or rounded lines, Empire or pre-Revolutionary styles with panniers and puffs, would prevail. The Marie Antoinette fichu of 1868–69 (second from right in No. 87) had long ends tied behind in a bow. Another style had a wide sash ending in a big bow at the back giving a puffed effect. Women wearing these dresses lent slightly forward in an attitude called for some obscure reason 'the Grecian bend'. A still more foolish affectation was the 'Alexandra limp' adopted by some admirers of the popular Princess of Wales, who was left slightly lame following a severe attack of rheumatic fever in 1867. Some of them even went so far as to have their shoes made with heels of unequal height![3] The celebrated 'man milliner' Worth made every effort to popularize panniers worn *without* a crinoline. Some Paris ball dresses of 1869 were practically historical costumes, suitable only for masquerades. This form of escapism led Princess Metternich and three other leaders of fashion to use sedan chairs! A year later the French defeat at Sedan marked the downfall of the Second Empire.

These fanciful costumes were not confined to the ballroom. 'New and elegant toilet for the beach, in the Louis XV style; dress made of emerald-green silk shot with white. The dress has two skirts, the first one being train-shaped and trimmed with gathered flounces, headed with a black velvet ribbon, crossed at regular distances by small pieces of the same ribbon. A similar ornamentation goes up twice on either side of the waist, and serves to hold up the second skirt, which is gathered and raised into a puff, much larger at the back than at the front. High bodice and short *paletot* without sleeves, trimmed to correspond with the dress.'[4] Anything more preposterously out of place than an elaborate silk dress with train trailing on the wet sand, it would be difficult to imagine. It is in fact doubtful whether such a dress as the one described was actually worn on the beach, though it may have been on the promenade. In England, at any rate, the French style was not received with much enthusiasm. When worn,

[1] ibid. 13 July 1867.   [2] ibid. 14 March 1868.
[3] 'Luke Limner' (John Leighton), *Madre Natura versus the Moloch of Fashion*, 2nd edition, 1874.
[4] *The Englishwoman's Domestic Magazine*, 1868.

panniers were moderate in size (No. 86), and crinolines, though smaller, continued to be used out of doors (No. 92). The obsession of the crinoline could not be easily forgotten, and although skirts could well have been as wide as was now the fashion over ordinary petticoats, the peculiar stiffness and swinging movement of the crinoline were still preferred. Perhaps English-women felt safer in their cages!

Indoors or in one's garden, the Empire gown predominated for a time, its straight classic lines being generally better suited to English taste and figures (Nos. 87, 89). This style might, one feels, well have become the dominating mode in reaction to the long reign of crinoline. Yet finally, voluptuous curves triumphed over classical verticals. The upper skirt was drawn up still higher and towards the back, where it developed into the bustle (1869–70) (No. 93), the petticoat becoming the main skirt. The dress was still worn over a kind of decadent small crinoline called 'crinolette', consisting of half-hoops at the back only, but the true crinoline was dead, and unmourned by those who had worn it so long.

For us, the swinging cage crinoline has such fascination that plays or operas set in the 'forties or early 'fifties are nearly always dressed ten to twenty years later. A few examples are *The Barretts of Wimpole Street*, *The Heiress* (based on Henry James's *Washington Square*), and *La Traviata*. We are now at a distance to appreciate the visual charm of this fashion, and no-one alive has had experience of its inconvenience. Yet until comparatively recent times detestation of the crinoline was the almost unanimous verdict of fashion historians.

As late as 1933 Herbert Norris made the sweeping statement: 'At no period in the history of costume have the clothes of men and women been so supremely hideous as those generally worn during the sixties and seventies of the nineteenth century.'[1] Twenty years earlier Julius M. Price called the crinoline 'the ugliest mode the world has probably ever seen'. Writing about the International Exhibition of 1862 he says: 'At this moment the crinoline, with all its hideous paraphernalia, was at the height of its absurdity, and the scenes witnessed in London amongst the crowds of visitors attracted by the Exhibition have been described as surpassing in pure extravagance of ugliness anything that had been seen before in the world of woman's dress.'[2] Octave Uzanne, author of many books on art and social subjects, wrote in 1898 of 'the monstrous caricature of the crinoline. . . . With the Second Empire we reach the

[1] Herbert Norris & Oswald Curtis, *Costume and Fashion*, Vol. VI, 'The Nineteenth Century', 1933.
[2] Julius M. Price, *Dame Fashion: Paris — London (1786–1912)*, London, 1913.

most hideous period in female dress that has ever vexed the artistic eye. We are face to face with a series of the most ungraceful, unbecoming, pretentious, and extravagant garments ever invented by the human brain . . . the frightful crinolines that swell every woman into a prop for yards of unnecessary stuff, the wide and ugly half sleeves, the screaming vulgarity of the colours, the thick stripes and heavy trimmings of all fashionable attire. It would be difficult indeed to discover more violent contrasts of colour, or shades more contrary to the law of harmony, than those which enjoyed so great favour during the Second Empire.'[1]

'Never has the crinoline furnished artistic models for painters', claimed Camille Piton quite erroneously just before World War I, ignoring — to mention only a few names — Boudin, Manet, Monet, as well as English anecdotal painters like W. P. Frith. 'It has always been attacked and never defended. We have never met anyone who defended this bizarre fashion, except the publishers of fashion papers.'[2]

[1] Octave Uzanne, *Fashion in Paris*, London, 1898.
[2] Camille Piton, *Le Costume Civil en France du XIII° au XIX° Siècle*, Paris, n.d. (1913).

PART II

Curves and Verticals

———————————————————————————————————————

'As the hermit-crab selects the shell of a whelk and grows to its shape, so does the modern dame — but no sooner has she acquired the desired form than fashion demands another', observed John Leighton,[1] the Victorian designer. Women — tired of wide skirts whether in the shape of domes, tea-cosies, bells, fans, funnels, lampshades, cones, or bottles — were turning eagerly to the development of curves with the aid of the bustle. Many were relieved that at last 'the dire calamity of the so-called crinoline mania'[2] was over.

Changes of fashion have an inconvenient way of not fitting in exactly with decades. The puff at the rear which was the outstanding feature of the early 'seventies had already begun to make its appearance in 1868, when Paris decreed that 'there shall be an abundance of crinoline, or bustle, or pannier, or tournure (for the bunch at the back goes by a variety of names) just below the waist'.[3]

In the first few years of the new decade the gathered-up overskirt supported by the bustle gave a bunched effect high up at the back (Nos. 99, 100, 102, 104, 111). Frequently the underskirt was trimmed with rows of stiffly pleated or kilted flounces (Nos. 98, 101). The bodice was rather short-waisted, with plain but not tight sleeves sometimes ending in a turned-back cuff or a ruffle, or else again in the old funnel shape of the 'fifties.

Unlike some revivals, the fashions of around 1870 really did have a certain likeness to those they imitated of nearly a hundred years earlier. Though inspired by the fashions of the early years of Louis XVI's reign, they were for some unaccountable reason designated Louis XV. After the death of Dickens in 1870 and the sale of the painting he had commissioned from W. P. Frith depicting the heroine of *Barnaby Rudge*, a special 'Dolly Varden' polonaise and

[1] 'Luke Limner' (John Leighton), *Madre Natura versus the Moloch of Fashion*, 1870.
[2] ibid.   [3] *The Queen*, 1868.

hat were designed in 1871, which, however, produced too great a resemblance to a rococo shepherdess to be in the best of taste.

The polonaise which was fashionable during much of the 'seventies was a revival of an eighteenth-century garment, consisting of a bodice and overskirt in one, the skirt being drawn back into an elaborate arrangement behind (No. 110).

Just as the main interest of the dress was concentrated on the curve of the bustle, the elaboration of the hair was also at the back, in a big chignon of plaits or curls (Nos. 102, 103, 104, 108). Hats and bonnets were tilted forward by this wen-like appendage (No. 97, 98, 101). It seems that in the late 'sixties and early 'seventies it was the hairdresser who forced the milliner's design, whereas in the mid-1920s it was the cloche hat that obliged even the most unwilling woman reluctantly to sacrifice her hair.

The more or less undisguised application of additional hair, even by young women, is a curious feature of the period, considering that a man with a *toupé* is always a figure of fun, since the abandonment of the decorative wig towards the close of the eighteenth century. 'The fashion of wearing false hair has become so universal', wrote Dr. Andrew Wynter, 'that the exception of the few persons content with the crop Nature has supplied simply serves to prove the rule. Those who do not adopt a whole chignon will wear part of one, or bring a simple plait into requisition. Even ladies who profess to scorn such additions insert a few surreptitious "frisettes" to shape their head-tire. These frisettes are made also of hair If we consider that even a moderate-sized "plait" contains as much hair as grows altogether on the head of an ordinary Englishwoman, and is probably half as long again, we may very reasonably be allowed to wonder whence the supply comes'[1] (Nos. 102, 103). The chief source was peasant girls in Germany, Italy, and France, who hardly missed their hair because they always wore traditional head-dresses. Hair was cut from prisoners, from paupers in the workhouse, and even — it was rumoured — from patients in fever hospitals and from corpses. Middle-class girls in need of money might sell their hair, like Jo March in 'Little Women'. In Catholic countries large quantities of hair came from novices entering convents. According to Challamel, street-sweepings of hair were sold to merchants.[2] English country people, on the other hand, were too superstitious to throw away their hair-combings, believing that if a magpie collected them to line his nest, the person from whom the hair came would surely die within a year.

[1] Dr Andrew Wynter, *Peeps into the Human Hive*, 1874.
[2] Augustin Challamel, *The History of Fashion in France*, 1882.

Curves and Verticals

About £100,000-worth of hair was annually imported into England and made up into finished goods sold at three times this price. Paris was, however, the main centre of making-up hair into fashionable chignons. In 1875 the manufacture of false hair in France amounted to 130,000 kilogrammes. Occasionally in Paris hair was dyed green, mauve, or blue, as it is today.

The use of false chignons must have been extremely annoying for the possessors of a splendid head of hair like the Empress Elisabeth of Austria (No. 88). As at all periods, many women of good position remained aloof from extreme fashions, and eschewed additional hair and exaggerated bustles (No. 105).

By 1873 the so-called Louis XV costume was said to be a thing of the past, though to us the general line looks very similar except that the bustle was slightly reduced in size and the skirt not quite so full (No. 107).

The following year appeared plain masculine-style jackets paving the way for a significant new fashion typical of the second half of the 'seventies: the cuirasse bodice (Nos. 109, 121, 123–4, 126–9, 131) — long-waisted, tight-fitting, and extending over the hips. It was practically a corset, made of shaped pieces of material with sometimes as many as seventeen seams so that it should tightly mould the curves of the body. 'To hide, yet to display, or rather to indicate and yet disclose, are the two objects of the bodice' explained Charles Blanc, the French art critic, remembering that Montaigne had written: 'There are certain things which are hidden in order to be shown.' And the former Director of the Beaux-Arts added with psychological insight: 'It must not be forgotten that often what is concealed is just that which is most wished to be displayed. The significance of the bodice results from this fact.'[1]

The decade of the 1870s was one of the most complex periods of fashion design. 'There is no such thing as a dress made of a single material' reported *The Queen*. Letting its readers into the secret of the latest fashions the magazine advised them to 'Take two materials, one of which shall represent the principal and the other the accessory, and out of these compose a costume, trimming the principal with the accessory and the accessory with the principal'.[2] Frequently the sleeves were of a different colour (Nos. 109, 111, 123, 126), and there might be a band set in down the middle of the back of the bodice, or a plastron inserted in its front to give a waistcoat effect. Strange combinations of materials and colours, and the temptation to apply too many pleatings, kiltings, flounces, ruchings, fringe and other ready-made trimmings often resulted in a confused and 'bitty' appearance, especially since flounces were themselves often trimmed with headings and edgings. Winter dresses trimmed with fringe gave the

[1] Charles Blanc, *Art and Ornament in Dress*, London, 1877.　　　[2] *The Queen*, 1877.

wearer an upholstered appearance (No. 110). Nevertheless, some dresses of the 'seventies are delightful for their grace and femininity. As time went on, subtler rules were devised for contrast in colour and texture: 'Dresses made of two or three materials are much less patchy in effect than when such combinations first came into favour. The bodice is now [1879] made of one fabric, the skirt of another, and trimmed with the material of the bodice.'[1] The latest scheme was to use a dull-surfaced and a glossy material of the same colour, or shades of the same colour. Olive and lime green, dark blue, cardinal red and striped materials, were all popular at this period. The pointed-toed cloth boots or shoes with kid under-leathers were supposed to harmonize with the prevailing tint of the costume or of its trimming.

Evening or dinner dresses often had elbow sleeves; ball dresses, tiny sleeves and a neckline low in front but fairly high behind. Twelve or fifteen button white kid gloves were worn, and shoes and stockings matched the dress. In 1877–78 ball dresses were trimmed with long trails of flowers (No. 124). Sometimes they were real blossoms, but artificial ones were worn in the hair — just the reverse of what would be practical. An incongruous accessory indoors — sometimes even with evening dress — was a small velvet muff decorated with an owl's head or even a whole bird. During this decade it became fashionable to wear a black velvet ribbon neck band, as depicted in the pictures of ballet dancers by Degas. They were forerunners, in England, of the wide jewelled 'dog collar' worn from the 1880s until the Great War, which had been fashionable in Paris as early as 1865.[2] It is worth pointing out that the women in photographs of the 'seventies rarely wear gloves, contrary to the rules of the etiquette books.

During the second half of the 'seventies it seemed as though women were growing taller and slimmer, more vertical, less curved — below the waist, at any rate. Whether they wore the cuirasse bodice or a Princess sheath dress, the effect was always figure-fitting to below the hips (Nos. 109, 110, 120, 121, 123–4, 126–9). By 1876 the bustle had disappeared, only an occasional bow at knee level behind acting as a vestigial reminder of its abundance. The skirt was tied back tightly by three or four ribbons inside, so that the front was stretched flat, though it might be trimmed with flounces or fringe. Behind, the skirt was draped and decorated in a variety of complicated ways, ending invariably in a train giving the wearer something of the appearance of a mermaid, or of a peacock trailing his folded tail (Nos. 107, 110, 111, 120, 121, 123–5). The train was intended to convey the impression that the wearer kept a carriage, but women who were not of the 'carriage class' trailed their appendages in the

[1] *The Queen*, 1879. [2] ibid. 1865.

street. Ruskin advised young women : 'You must not buy yards of useless stuff to make a knot or flounce, nor drag them behind you over the ground. And your walking dress must never touch the ground at all. I have lost much of the faith I once had in the common sense and personal delicacy of the present race of average Englishwomen, by seeing how they will allow their dresses to sweep the streets, if it is the fashion to be scavengers.'[1]

G. F. Watts also deplored 'the persistent tendency to suggest that the most beautiful half of humanity is furnished with tails. Yet amid the constant changes of fashion this strange peculiarity is almost as constantly preserved.'[2] His essay having been written in 1882, it is difficult to be certain that Watts was complaining of trains, which by this time had been given up except for evening wear. On the other hand, the revival of the bustle was only just beginning to make itself felt in London.

Margaret Oliphant, the novelist and historical writer, agreed heartily with Ruskin's and Watts's objections. 'Nothing can be a more certain indication that the wearer of a long train is not a lady, than the fact that she allows it to sweep the street behind her.' From the artistic point of view, she approved of trained dresses at home. 'As for the long skirt indoors, it is not a thing which ever will be abolished, or aught to be abolished, in our opinion. It is graceful and dignified in itself; it belongs to the fundamental idea of women's apparel, and possesses all the poetical and symbolical qualities which are necessary to a noble and fine ideal of dress. So long as it sweeps over carpets, or polished floors, clean and carefully kept, or over the cleanest of all carpets, a luxurious and well-mown lawn, it has all the elements of beauty, and is not more inconvenient than a beautiful thing may be permitted to be.'[3]

Mrs. Oliphant advocated special clothes for walking, boating, and lawn tennis. 'Men play this game in all the ease of "flannels", while women — or let us say girls — for few beyond that stage of existence are tempted to throw themselves into amusement of this kind — seldom do more in the way of "change" than to add the frippery of a lawn tennis apron to a dress perhaps, but not always, a little shorter and simpler than ordinary' (Nos. 116, 118). *Punch* mocked at this fashion by illustrating men tennis players handicapped by having their legs tied together with a scarf to put them on a par with their feminine opponents. Women were, indeed, terribly restricted in their movements by the tied-back skirt, which was referred to frankly as 'the single trouser'. 'No-one but a woman knows how her dress twists around her knees,

[1] John Ruskin, *Fors Clavigera*, 1876.
[2] G. F. Watts, 'On Taste in Dress', *The Nineteenth Century*, January, 1883.
[3] Mrs. Margaret Oliphant, *Dress*, Art at Home Series, London, 1878.

121 *A lady, by Hills & Saunders, Oxford, c. 1877*

120 *A lady, by Theodor Prümm, Berlin, 1878–9*

123 *A lady, by Fratelli Vianelli, Venice, c. 1878*

122 *Miss Ada Dyas, by Horatio Nelson King, London,*
c. 1875

125 *Ball dress, by F. Gutekunst, Philadelphia, c. 1877*

124 *Ball dress, c. 1877–3*

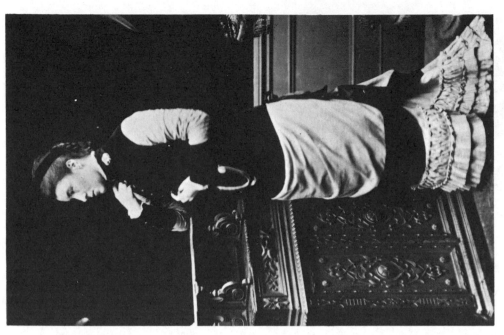

127   *A lady, by E. T. Church, Belfast, c. 1879*

126   *A lady, c. 1879*

128 *Winston Churchill and his aunt, Dublin, 1880*

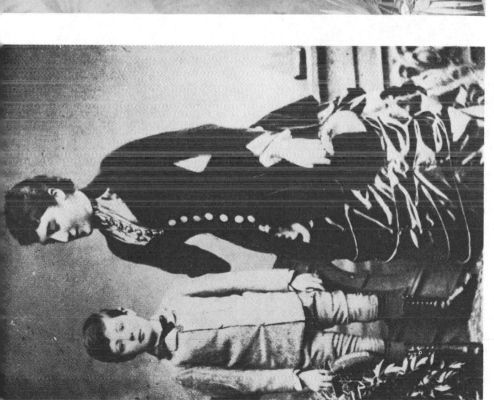

129 *The Countess of Dudley and her daughter, by W. & D. Downey, London, c. 1880*

131 *Lady in Court dress, by Window & Grove, London,*
c. 1880

130 *Oscar Wilde in America in 1882*

132　*Marriage of a daughter of the Duke of Buckingham (on right) at Stowe House, c. 1883*

133 *Picnicking by the Thames, by William Taunt, c.* 1883

134 *Scarborough, by G. W. Wilson, c. 1884*

135   *Queen Louise of Denmark and her granddaughters.*
Athens, August 1882

136   *Miss Coleman jumping, by Eadweard Muybridge,*
Philadelphia, 1885

137   *Mrs Finney, by Lord Walter Campbell, c. 1884*

138   *Mrs. Langtry, by Lafayette, London, c. 1888*

139 *Four women at Portelet Bay, Jersey, c.* 1889

140 *Paddling at Skipness, c.* 1883

141   *American tennis club, c.* 1887

142   *Tricycling, c.* 1884

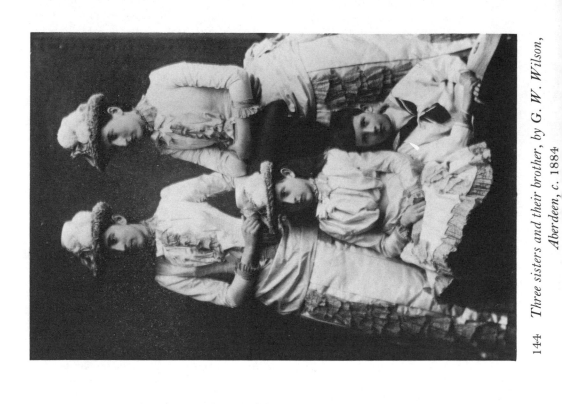

144 *Three sisters and their brother, by G. W. Wilson, Aberdeen, c. 1884*

143 *Miss Burnett, by G. W. Wilson, Aberdeen, c. 1884*

146 Lady Brooke (later Countess of Warwick), by
Herbert Barraud, London, c. 1886

145 Princess Beatrice and Prince Henry of Battenberg,
by Elliott & Fry, London, 1885

148 *Miss Young, c. 1884*

147 *Venus, c. 1887*

150   *Miss Leila Johnston, 1885*

149   *A lady, by G. W. Wilson, Aberdeen, c. 1839*

151, 152 *Military style costumes photographed by G. W. Wilson of Aberdeen, 1885 and 1888-9*

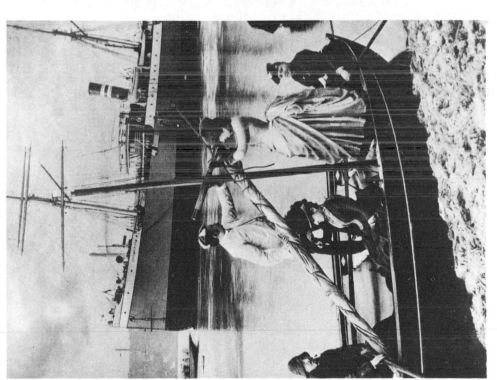

154   *Horace Hutchinson in golf suit, by Walery, London, 1889*

153   *Hamburg harbour, by Srna, Vienna, c. 1886*

155   *Skating in Vienna*, by Oscar Van Zel, c. 1887

156 *A party of tourists crossing the Mer de Glace near Chamonix, c. 1885*

158 *Princess Victoria of Wales at Frogmore, 1889,*
photographed by the Princess of Wales

157 *Princess Louise, Duchess of Fife, at her Scottish*
home Mar Lodge by W. & D. Downey, September, 1889

159   *Tea by the Thames near Cliveden, c. 1888–9*

161 *Miss Julia Neilson, by Walery, London, c. 1887*

160 *Mr. and Mrs. Gladstone with Lord Rendel and his daughters at Naples, January 1889*

162   *Domestic interior, by Robert Slingsby, Norwich,* 1889

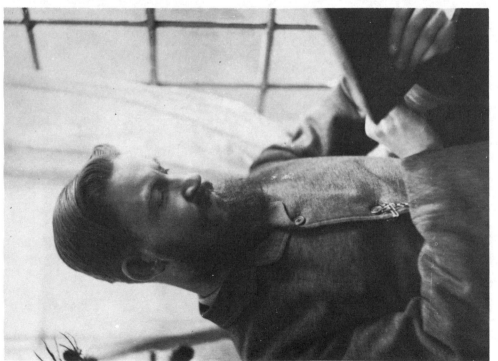

163   George Bernard Shaw, by Frederick Hollyer, London, c. 1890

164   Oscar Wilde, by W. & D. Downey, London, 1890

166 *Lord and Lady Rendel, their daughters, son-in-law Mr. Goodhart and grandchild. September 1890*

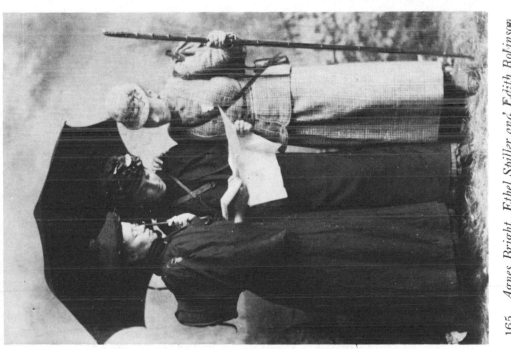

165 *Agnes Bright, Ethel Spiller and Edith Robinson setting out on a walking tour, c. 1890*

167   *The Duchess of Albany with her children, nieces and nephews.*
Claremont, April 1890

168   *Woman with little boy in Scottish dress on a donkey, c.* 1893

169   *Aubrey Beardsley, by Frederick Holyer, c. 1894*

170   *Mrs. Saxton Noble tricycling, c. 1893*

172   *The Duchess Maximilian of Bavaria, by*
Dittmar, Munich, 1892

171   *The Kaiserin Augusta Victoria, consort of*
Kaiser Wilhelm II, 1891

174 *Lady Randolph Churchill, by W. & D. Downey,*
London, 1893

173 *Princess Marie of Edinburgh and her fiancé*
Prince Ferdinand of Rumania, June 1892

175   *Girls in cycling bloomers on the quay at Boulogne, 1897*

176   *Coney Island, N.Y., c. 1899*

doubles her fatigue, and arrests her locomotive powers' moaned Mrs. Oli-phant, regretting the demise of the short walking dress of the 'sixties. 'It [the crinoline] offended every law of beauty and every instinct of grace; but there was comfort in it.'

At the time of Mrs. Oliphant's protest, *costumes de fatigue* with a simple pleated skirt two inches short of the ground were designed for visiting the Paris international exhibition of 1878. Clothes on these lines, in warmer materials, were worn for shooting — or rather joining the guns for lunch — yachting, and other sporting activities. In this way the tailor-made suit for women made its debut. The Jersey costume introduced in 1879 and popularized by the Jersey Lily, Mrs. Langtry, at the Cowes Regatta, consisted of a long tight-fitting plain jersey of 'elastic' woven material and a kilted untrained skirt with a functionless sash draped loosely round at knee-level. Its chief novelty lay in the stretching qualities of the jersey bodice which fitted like a glove, without being in any way stiffened, and was thus fairly practical for tennis and other games. Nevertheless, many women continued to play in ordinary clothes.

In the late 'seventies many English intellectuals turned against conventional fashions and, aiming at Pre-Raphaelitism in dress, pursued the artistic in a rather self-conscious way. The reform movement, which was not connected with the original Pre-Raphaelite Brotherhood founded in 1848, saw its ideal in 'the forms of dress — simple without bareness, complex without confusion — and the colours, harmonious however varied, which marked, roughly speaking, the period of Edward III's reign from 1327 to 1377'.[1] William Morris pre-ferred the thirteenth century; his dictum that 'No dress can be beautiful that is stiff; drapery is essential' applies to both equally.

The first aim of the Pre-Raphaelite woman was to have an 'antique' waist — rather broad and in the natural position. Her skirts were loose enough for her to 'sit down or walk upstairs at will, unlike some votaries of the present fashions' For social occasions she did not disdain a flowing train — though not one of the fashionable fan-tail type. In reaction against the straight narrow sleeves that had been so long in fashion, the aesthetic woman invented loose sleeves of varied design — many being puffed or slashed in Renaissance style, rather than fourteenth-century Gothic. Some of them, full from shoulder to elbow, are a pointer to the enormous balloon sleeves of the mid-'nineties. Colour schemes were the 'indescribable tints' advocated by Ruskin: deep red, soft bluish-green, greenish-brown, dull orange, amber — in short, the 'greenery-yallery, Grosvenor Gallery' colours satirized by W. S. Gilbert in *Patience* (1881).

[1] Mary Eliza Haweis, *The Art of Dress*, 1879.

To the aesthete, even more than to the woman of fashion, dress was a means of self-expression. 'In nothing are character and perception so insensibly but inevitably displayed', wrote Mrs. Haweis, 'as in dress, and taste in dress. Dress is the second self, a dumb self, yet a most eloquent expositer of the person. Dress bears the same relation to the body as speech does to the brain; and therefore dress may be called the speech of the body.'[1]

'I hope the day will soon come when it will no longer be a slur on a good woman, old or young, to say "she thinks a great deal of dress; she attaches enormous importance to aesthetics". A foolish shame traceable to old Huguenot feeling survives, about some vague wrongness in trying to improve the looks, and a fossilized prejudice against "vanity". A pretty face is such a delight to the eye that it ought to be prized and cultivated. Do then your best with the body; and next, do your best with its covering.'[2]

These are scarcely sentiments that one would expect from a Victorian clergyman's wife, but worldly Mrs. Haweis was hardly a characteristic example, any more than the Rev. Hugh Reginald Haweis was a typical churchman of the period.

A competent painter and exhibitor at the Royal Academy, Mrs. Haweis was one of the earliest exponents of Pre-Raphaelitism in dress. In order to make sure that the colour of her dress would not clash with the interior decoration, she used to make a preliminary visit to any house to which she was invited to a party.

Unlike most of her contemporaries in England, Mrs. Haweis defended the use of make-up, feeling that an unnecessary amount of contempt and contumely was cast on cosmetics, in which she saw 'no more harm or degradation in avowedly hiding defects of complexion, or touching the face with pink or white, than in padding the dress, piercing the ears, or replacing a lost tooth'. She equally frankly admitted having no prejudice against false hair used 'in moderation and *when necessary*', exemplifying her point by adding: 'When a plait is palpably bigger than one human head can supply, it ceases to be an ornament, and becomes a burden and annoyance.'[3]

Watts was one of the many artists who held that the coiffure should not materially increase the apparent size of the head, and came down heavily against additional hair. 'It may be laid down as a rule in dressing the hair, and in all other dressing, that all that is false is in bad taste, and a lady should be as unwilling to wear false hair as she would be to wear false jewels.'[4] Having been

[1] Mary Eliza Haweis, *The Art of Beauty*, 1878.   [2] ibid.
[3] Mary Eliza Haweis, *The Art of Dress*, 1879.
[4] G. F. Watts, 'On Taste in Dress', *The Nineteenth Century*, Jan. 1883.

used all his life to the centre parting in women's hair, he found it particularly objectionable to part the hair on one side, 'such disturbance of the balance being unnatural, the two sides of all organic structures always corresponding even in what is purely ornamental; and it is a safe rule to make, that what is unnatural is not in good taste.'[1]

With an air of finality *The Englishwoman's Domestic Magazine* declared in 1876 false hair a thing of the past. Nevertheless, the long ringlets sometimes worn hanging down the back, especially in evening dress (No. 125) were sometimes additions, and for several decades women often wore a false fringe of curls in order to avoid cutting their front hair short (No. 146). On the whole, however, the natural hair was worn dressed fairly close, curled, and piled towards the back of the top of the head. In this position was perched the hat or bonnet (No. 109), for the idea of covering the head had given place to the desire to adorn it. 'A bonnet', wrote Charles Blanc, 'is simply an excuse for a feather, a pretext for a spray of flowers, the support for an aigrette, the fastening for a plume of Russian cocks' feathers. It is placed on the head, not to protect it, but that it may be seen better. Its great use is to be charming.'[2] As opposed to bonnets, hats were often tilted forward, and in 1877 the Gainsborough hat was introduced, made of velvet or plush, with curved brim and a feather, put on with a rakish sideways tilt (No. 121). The fact that it had a brim at all made it seem large in comparison with bonnets, though it was very far from the wide hat of the Duchess of Devonshire and other ladies in Gainsborough's portraits. The Gainsborough hat found favour with the aesthetes, who refused to spend a couple of guineas on a trivial bonnet. 'A wired edifice of tulle and velvet', opined Mrs. Haweis, '(two materials that, from their contrast, do not easily mix well) trimmed with a mass of valueless blond [lace], a spray of tinsel, and perhaps a bird's-nest or something else equally bad in taste — e.g. moths, beetles, lizards, mice &c. — can never be a beautiful object. At present the bonnets and the brains they cover are too often not unfit combinations.'[3] Indoors, caps were now only worn with a teagown; otherwise they were relegated to old ladies.

During the late 'seventies the volume of underclothing had to be greatly reduced on account of the tight-fitting skirts. What remained, was shaped to the figure, and instead of flannel or linen, was made of thin washing-silk, sometimes even coloured instead of white, which was considered very fast. According to the censorious Uzanne, around 1880 'the last remains of feminine

[1] ibid.
[2] Charles Blanc, *Art and Ornament in Dress*, 1877.
[3] Mary Eliza Haweis, *The Art of Beauty*, 1878.

modesty sunk out of sight, drowned by the prevalent mania for elaborate underclothing'.[1]

A liking for horizontal trimming or drapery on the skirt, evident in 1878–79 (No. 126) became intensified in the early 'eighties. Below the wasp waist the narrow skirt of even length all round and with horizontal trimming looked like half a Christmas cracker (No. 131). The bodice had an hour-glass form like the wooden Noah's Ark figures which escaped the Sunday ban on toys on account of the biblical subject. After about 1882 the plain high-necked bodices were not quite so long as in the 'seventies, and instead of being laced up the back, most of them fastened with a row of buttons down the front (Nos. 137, 140). Sleeves were long, plain and tight. All the interest lay in the skirt, which usually had pleats or folds round the thighs, or a scarf, or a double 'fishwife' skirt with the upper part caught up like an apron (Nos. 137, 142, 144–5, 151, 153). The underskirt was often kilted. The general line of the 'eighties looks like a harder version of the 'seventies. The combination of plain tight bodice and complicated skirt giving a 'plain above, fancy below' appearance was still there, but instead of gentle curves there were now stiff lines. In the second half of the decade, particularly, women appear aggressively erect and square-shouldered, often holding a hefty umbrella in front of them like a weapon (Nos. 157, 158). (Sunshades, on the other hand, were often very pretty, with a flounce all round the edge (No. 134)). It was a striking change from the attitude of their grandmothers in the 'forties. There was even a fashion for dresses in the style of a military uniform (Nos. 151, 152).

No trains were worn in the day-time, but persisted as a separate attachment with full evening dress, which in 1880 was 'short', i.e. shoe length (No. 131), the wearing of silver and gold anklets being considered 'the *ne plus ultra* of distinction and elegance'.[2] Some dresses between 1879 and 1883 had low panniers at thigh level (No. 140) giving a totally different effect from the original eighteenth-century panniers or their revival in the late 'sixties.

In spring 1880 it was confidently announced that 'Dress improvers, worn in Paris as a matter of course, are coming in here'.[3] In fact it was not until summer 1882, after a smooth-hipped vertical period of eight years, that a small proportion of English dresses were worn with the revived bustle. At first it was quite small, but before 1885 it was clear that the vertical had been defeated by the curve in the first round of the Battle of the Bulge. The new tournure was situated several inches lower than the bustle of the early 'seventies, was narrower, and jutted out horizontally, giving the wearer rather the shape of a hen (Nos. 145, 146, 148, 150, 153). Not unreasonably, a Turkish lady whose

---

[1] Octave Uzanne, *Fashion in Paris*, 1898.   [2] *Le Follet*, 1880.   [3] *The Queen*, 1880.

curiosity got the better of her manners asked the British Ambassador's wife in Constantinople : 'Are *all* the ladies in your country deformed like you ?'

Because of the protuberance, skirts had to be considerably wider. The upper skirt was draped in various ways, sometimes diagonally, with a 'waterfall back' of broad vertical unpressed pleats falling over the bustle. In the latter part of the decade ball dresses often had a skirt at the back opening over a front one of different material, and this back skirt formed a train from the waist. With the light materials of evening or visiting dresses falling loosely over the tournure, the effect was more attractive than with cloth morning dresses, under which the bustle produced a peculiarly stiff appearance (Nos. 145, 148, 153, 155, 157).

Tournures were made in a variety of complicated constructions, in silk, cashmere, flannel, and muslin, often trimmed outside with lace. They had four or five graduated steels four inches apart, each one longer than the last, kept in place by a lacing or elastic at the back. Others were made of woven wire like a sieve, with a pad or small cushion on top. For Queen Victoria's Golden Jubilee celebrations a patriotic inventor patented a bustle containing a musical box which played 'God Save the Queen' whenever the wearer sat down — an exhausting device, for naturally she had immediately to rise again, and every one else with her!

During both bustle periods, mantles, *visites*, and other wraps were often made with a division at the back to allow for the tournure; otherwise they had ample pleats.

Daytime materials were on the whole rather heavy, giving an upholstered look to the tight bodice. Tight-lacing — unnecessary during the crinoline period when the width of the skirt made the waist look small by contrast — became in the 'seventies, and remained for many years, probably more severe than at any other period. The discomfort of this led to the introduction of loose teagowns in the late 'seventies, in which married women — but not girls — could relax for the new habit of five o'clock tea. Mrs. Oliphant rightly observed that 'the majority of the costumes adopted by humankind are cunningly devised upon principles which secure more or less constant discomfort to the wearers'. Modern women, of course, are still far from having attained complete comfort : nylon stockings give no protection in winter, and too narrow shoes with stiletto heels severely limit the capacity for walking. However, they have the consolation that even if crippled by the time they reach middle age, at least they will not actually die in the cause of fashion, which literally happened in some cases of tight-lacing. The fashionable hermit-crab had indeed to grow to the shape of her shell with a vengeance. It was not only a matter of the corset crushing the body while being worn; the internal organs were forced permanently out of position, resulting in serious illness and sometimes even leading directly to death. The lower ribs, too, grew quite out of place and stuck into the lungs. (Sir) Frederick Treves was one of innumerable medical men who campaigned against tight-lacing, heavy trailing skirts, and pointed high-heeled shoes. Doctors were also against the habit of turning the toes out — seldom seen today — which arose from dancing masters' notions of elegance, and was a common cause of weak ankles and flat feet.

In 1878, during his last term at Oxford, Oscar Wilde declared that reformation of dress was of far greater importance than reformation of religion. He inveighed against tight-lacing both from the aesthetic and the health point of view. Artistically, he considered it 'a great error to imagine that an unnaturally small waist gives an air of grace, or even slightness, to the whole figure. Its effect, as a rule, is simply to exaggerate the width of the shoulder and the hips. . . . Fashion's motto is "Il faut souffrir pour être belle"; but the motto of art and of commonsense is "Il faut être bête pour souffrir".'[1] Wilde advocated dresses suspended from the shoulders, obviating the need for a corset, and he reviled 'that modern monstrosity, the so-called "dress improver".'

Many writers have emphatically stated that Victorian women achieved an 18-inch or even a 17-inch waist. This I could never believe. Mrs. Doris Langley Moore has disproved it by simply showing how tiny a circle of 17-inch circumference is.[2] My assumption that such measurements gave the nominal size of the corset, making no allowance for the gap across which the laces go, is borne out by a booklet published by a firm of corset manufacturers. The author settles the matter beyond dispute : 'A distinction should be made between *actual* and *corset* measurements, because stays, as ordinarily worn, do not meet at the back. Young girls, especially, derive intense satisfaction from proclaiming the diminutive size of their corset. Many purchase 18 and 19 inch stays, who must leave them open 2, 3 and 4 inches.'[3]

This firm, E. M. Ward & Co. of Bradford, were agents for Dr. Gustav Jaeger's sanitary woollen clothing. It was owing to this German crank that the fad for wearing wool arose in the 'eighties, which persisted for well over a generation. I still remember the childhood misery of tickly Jaeger combinations, which one hot spring day I threw out of my bedroom window, demanding indignantly of my mother : 'What do you expect me to wear?' Unfortunately it was windy as well as warm, and the offending garment drifted into the

[1] Oscar Wilde, 'Slaves of Fashion', n.d., pub. in *Art & Decoration*, 1920.
[2] Doris Langley Moore, *The Woman in Fashion*, 1949.
[3] *The Dress Reform Problem*, Bradford, 1886.

next-door neighbour's garden, where I was sent shamefacedly to retrieve it.

Dr. Jaeger, Professor of Zoology at Stuttgart University, found many disciples amongst English medical men, who supported his — to me, at any rate — uncomfortable theory that woollen underclothing is the most healthy kind in all circumstances. They even made the nonsensical claim that in hot weather wool is cooler than any other material because it does not conduct the heat of the atmosphere to the body. Wool became an absolute craze, initially in intellectual circles. G. B. Shaw bought a complete Jaeger outfit of brown knitted wool, and another of silver-grey woollen stockinet (No. 163). Legend has it that on a country walk with Shaw, Lord Olivier complained that the friction of his companion's swinging arms against this material made a chirping noise like a cricket, loud enough to drown their conversation.[1]

Wearing Jaeger underwear, and flannel body-belts in addition, people played tennis and went on summer walking tours. Inevitably they collapsed from heat apoplexy, which they called sunstroke, and wrapped themselves in extra shawls to cool down slowly. Dr. Jaeger's Sanitary Woollen System was considered particularly suitable for cycling. An imperative rule was that 'every garment worn whilst cycling should be of flannel or woollen material, without any admixture of cotton or linen in any form. Sore throat is often to be traced to the linen band which so many tailors and shirtmakers will fit round the neck of a flannel shirt, whilst there is often in addition a little square of linen marked with the maker's name and address, which, when it is damp, can be readily felt.'[2] Mrs. Ada S. Ballin recommended for female tricyclists, 'neat dark cloth costumes lined with woollen material, and the ideal way of wearing them is with woollen combinations next the skin, a flannel body [bodice] fitting closely to the figure to take the place of stays, and buttoned to this a pair of knickerbockers or trousers of cloth to match the dress. Of course, these un-mentionables do not show, but a lady clothed in this way is better able to face the risks of an accident than one in petticoats.'[3]

An outfit rather similar in appearance to the one in No. 142 won a prize at the National Health Society's exhibition in 1883. The skirt could be unfastened to make room for the action of the knees when riding; when buttoned up, bows of ribbon hid the join. Another tricycling costume had a flounce on the front and side breadths of an ordinary walking skirt; the flounce was buttoned up when walking, and let down to conceal the feet when on the machine. How women could undertake any activity in these thick, tight and heavy clothes is beyond

[1] Frank Harris, *Bernard Shaw*, 1931.
[2] Viscount Bury and G. Lacy Hillier, *Cycling*, 1887.
[3] Ada S. Ballin, *Health and Beauty in Dress*, 3rd edition, n.d. (1893).

71

comprehension. Coolness was obviously no consideration, whether for sport or otherwise. 'Fashion has decreed that, by married women at all events, mantles must be worn even in hot weather.'[1]

In 1880 Viscountess Harberton founded the Rational Dress Society 'to promote the adoption of a style of dress based upon considerations of health, comfort and beauty'.[2] Apart from campaigning against tight-lacing, hampering skirts, and high heels, one of the Society's aims was 'to recommend that the maximum weight of underclothing (without shoes) should not exceed 7 lbs.'! In contrast, letter-scales would be necessary to record the infinitesimal weight of modern underclothes. Folds of drapery round the legs, objected Lady Harberton, were only suitable for statues which have 'nothing much to do beyond leaning against balustrades and being calm'. Women ought to wear a divided skirt, instead of hanging a kind of curtain round their legs.

Lady Harberton's dress reform ideas were supported on medical grounds by the assistant surgeon at the London Hospital, (Sir) Frederick Treves, who naïvely believed that personal adornment was only a *minor* object in dress. Describing Lady Harberton's rational dress, Treves could not bring himself to refer to 'legs' or 'trousers', but explained that 'each limb is separately clothed by its own "skirt". By an ingenious arrangement of material, however, the division between the two limbs is scarcely obvious.'[3] In fact the rational dress was a fairly normal-looking tailor-made suit, but without a wasp waist, and with a draped tunic over the wide 'divided skirt' or knickerbockers, which were hardly noticeable. The members of the Rational Dress Society were fully alive to the fact that 'the effect of singularity in attire is to incur a social martyrdom out of all proportion to the relief obtained. It is vain to be comfortably and modestly attired if one is to be made an object of observation or ridicule.'[4] Hence the draperies with which most of the dress reformers disguised their divided skirts.

Mrs. Oscar Wilde, an active member of the Society, campaigned in lectures against the tightness of clothes, shoes, and gloves, the unnecessary weight of dresses and cloaks, and for the divided skirt. Her husband approved of it in principle, but he wanted it to be honest. 'If the divided skirt is to be of any positive value, it must give up all idea of "being identical in appearance with an ordinary skirt". The moment it imitates a dress it is lost; but let it visibly announce itself as what it actually is, and it will go far towards solving a real difficulty.'[5]

[1] *The Lady's World*, 1887.
[2] Viscountess Harberton, *Reasons for Reform in Dress*, n.d. (c. 1882).
[3] (Sir) Frederick Treves, *The Influence of Clothing on Health*, n.d. (1886).
[4] *The Rational Dress Society's Gazette*, Sept. 1888.
[5] Oscar Wilde, 'More Radical Ideas upon Dress Reform', *The Pall Mall Gazette*, 11 Nov. 1884.

Oscar Wilde recommended 'a substratum of pure wool, such as is supplied by Dr. Jaeger under the modern German system (i.e. combinations with long sleeves and legs)'. It is extremely difficult to visualize Constance Wilde in long woollen combinations, and Wilde's comedies are so much concerned with the world of fashion that his advocacy of dress reform from the health as well as the aesthetic point of view may come as a surprise to many readers.

Men's clothes also came under fire during Oscar Wilde's lecture tour of the United States in 1882. Clad in late eighteenth-century style (No. 130) he inveighed against modern dress. 'We have lost all nobility of dress, and in doing so, have almost annihilated the modern sculptor. . . . To see the frock-coat of the drawing room done in bronze, or the double waistcoat perpetuated in marble [on monuments] adds a new horror to death.'[1]

Oscar Wilde advocated 'some modification of the Greek costume' worn over Jaeger combinations. Yet, as Mrs. Oliphant had already rightly pointed out, it would be more possible to disestablish the Church, abolish the House of Lords, and cut the sacred vesture of the British Constitution into little pieces, than to translate English garments into Greek. The suggestion is a very good example of the impracticable character of almost all projects of clothes reform.'[2]

Many active young women liked man-tailored suits, even if they did not go so far as to wear 'bifurcated garments'. The tailor-made was practical for women needing neat clothes that would not get spoilt easily. By the early eighties a number of careers were open to women, including that standard job for the middle-class, typewriting. The Ladies' Typewriting and General Copying Office advertised in 1885 the copying of documents for solicitors, authors' MSS, actor's parts, etc., on Remington machines (introduced in 1878). 'A good typewriter [a woman, not a Remington] ought to be able to earn 25s. a week.' Female compositors had existed since 1840; twenty years later Emily Faithfull started the Victoria Press especially for the employment of women; women found work as telegraph operators from 1870 on, and the opening of the first telephone exchange in Britain nine years later offered them further opportunities, as did the Post Office Savings Bank in 1881.

For the convenience of the professional woman working in London, the A.B.C. chain of teashops started in 1880, and four years later the Ladies' Lavatory Company opened its first establishment at Oxford Circus.

There was considerable prejudice against emancipated women and 'strong minded females' — an old expression still current in 1886 to denote, for

[1] Oscar Wilde, lecture on 'The Practical Application of the Principles of the Aesthetic Theory to Exterior and Interior House Decoration, with Observations upon Dress and Personal Ornaments'. Pub. in *Essays and Lectures by Oscar Wilde*, 6th edition, London, 1928.
[2] Margaret Oliphant, *Dress*, 1878.

example, women who studied at Universities or read at the British Museum. Before the building of the North Library, the British Museum Reading Room was seriously overcrowded, a fact for which the increased number of female readers was of course blamed. A peevish mysogonist complained in *The St. James's Gazette* that women disturbed him by rustling their dresses; besides, he could no longer shake the ink from his pen on to the floor, for fear of spoiling their clothes. A girl student retaliated by complaining of old men who wasted valuable space by dozing at the reading-desks — as they still do.

Older women, too, were livelier at this period than they used to be. 'In the past generations, matrons of forty resigned themselves to caps and sank contentedly into middle age; now those of that age play lawn tennis and dance as lightly as their daughters.'[1]

In the 1880s the tailor-made — largely due to Redfern — became high fashion, and those made of fine cloth could be worn even at quiet weddings. English tailor-mades were eagerly bought by Continental women and Americans. In most of them only the plain bodices fall in line with our idea of a tailor-made suit; the skirts were elaborately draped (No. 137, 142, 145).

Correct accessories were doeskin, chamois, or suede gloves (not kid), and plain boots with heels of moderate height. A stiff 'boater' of the kind long worn at Cowes was the proper headgear in summer; otherwise a felt hat of rather masculine shape, called a 'Fedora' after the heroine of a play by Victorien Sardou in which Sarah Bernhardt scored a triumph in 1882. French bonnets were too dressy with a tailor-made.

In the early 'eighties brimmed hats were worn in summer (Nos. 140, 142, 144) as well as tiny bonnets (Nos. 129, 132), then came Olivia bonnets (named after the daughter of the Vicar of Wakefield) going up to a gable shape in front, and extremely high-crowned hats shaped like a flower-pot (No. 157). They were less attractively trimmed than in the 'seventies, being sometimes decked with whole owls or other birds, or bright-winged beetles — worn, surprisingly, by the aesthetic Mrs. Oscar Wilde at a Grosvenor Gallery private view in 1887. 'On some of the sealskin toques and hats are to be seen tiny cubs of bears, or baby squirrels, which seem to be playing hide and seek among the wings and bows.'[2] In summer 1887, bizarre Paris hat trimmings included carrots, turnips and beetroot, as well as the slightly more orthodox plums, pears and peaches, besides stuffed birds — whole parrots, lovebirds, finches, blackbirds, and pigeons.[3] To what extent such freakish and tasteless trimmings were worn is problematical. I can only say that in all the thousands of

[1] *The Woman's World*, edited by Oscar Wilde, 1888.
[2] *The Lady's World*, winter 1886. [3] *The Lady's World*, 1887.

photographs which I have studied, nothing more eccentric appears than currants on a bonnet of the late 'seventies (No. 109) and the seagulls in Nos. 212 and 216 — the last thing one would expect on a suffragette. As so often happens, the fashion and the reality were not synonymous.

The palm for perversity in ornaments must go to a muff with a kitten's head on it.[1] In fancy jewellery, too, the craze for zoological specimens in the 'eighties is bewildering : brooches in the form of a bumble-bee, an emerald caterpillar, a gold spider, a diamond chicken in an enamelled egg, a silver water-rat on a gilt reed, chased by a duck.[2]

As the 'eighties progressed, the day bodice became a little longer, sometimes with a deep point reminiscent of the 'forties. Frequently it turned back with revers, had a simulated waistcoat (Nos. 142, 147) or a real one (Nos. 151, 152). The upstanding collar was at least two inches high, and the plain narrow sleeves, which previously had usually been full length, often ended well above the wrist by 1887 (No. 149). The skirt had now a straighter line, usually undraped, and from 1887 on, often without the former typical horizontal scarf. Sometimes a panel of different material or embroidery decorated the front (No. 149) or the skirt opened to display an underskirt (Nos. 138, 162) but there were still plenty of skirts with a draped apron effect.

In this decade full-length fur coats were introduced. The majority were of sealskin, though sable was particularly prized, and was used to border Mrs. Gladstone's seal coat (No. 160).

For six years from 1879 the most usual hair style was comparatively simple, giving a small head. The hair was dressed in plaits or a twist low at the back, with a fringe, usually curled, on the forehead (Nos. 131, 138, 146, etc.). In the second half of the 'eighties many women arranged their hair scraped up in a knot on top (Nos. 147, 161), with a tuft of flowers or feathers in the evening.

Little girls were dressed in a sophisticated way like adults (No. 129), and even wore a bustle for 'best'. The black stockings and solid buttoned boots, looking too clumsy for their elaborate frocks (No. 135) were a kind still worn in the twentieth century (No. 196).

It was in the late 'eighties that the famous Little Lord Fauntleroy suit came into fashion. Frances Hodgson Burnett's story was published in 1886, and for many years little Cedric's Cavalier-style black velvet suit with a lace collar, and long curls, was inflicted on boys. The fashion for sailor suits (Nos. 144, 167) lasted from the mid-'sixties right through the Edwardian period, when it was intensified by naval rivalry between England and Germany. Edward VII had worn a sailor suit as early as 1847 for a portrait by Winterhalter. Highland

---

[1] *The Queen*, 1883.   [2] ibid. 1884.

costume was also still much worn by small boys at this period (No. 167). A plainer and more suitable get-up for older boys was the Norfolk suit, or a simple lounge jacket and knickerbockers, but often a kind of Eton suit and top hat were inflicted on them.

Men's lounge jackets lost something of their easy, sack look around 1870, when they were cut with a rounded curve at the bottom and closer fitting. For a few years the morning coat, too — which in the later 'seventies and 'eighties tended to displace the frock coat for many functions, even society weddings (No. 132) — was cut away in a stronger curve, revealing the bottom of the waistcoat, and was shorter than before. After 1876, coats of all types were longer. Whether only the top button, or (in the later 'seventies and early 'eighties) several buttons were fastened, the lapels always closed high, offering small scope for waistcoats and neckties. The 'dress lounge' — which we call dinner jacket — was introduced in England in 1888 for informal evening parties at which no ladies were present, and for dinner in country houses. It was the invention of some American millionaires at Tuxedo Park, N.Y., who wanted to be informal and comfortable amongst themselves.[1]

For tennis men usually wore white or light-coloured knickerbockers (No. 118) which began to be replaced during the 'eighties by white trousers. It was not done — in England, at any rate — to play tennis in a lounge suit (No. 141). White trousers were also correct for boating, with a striped jacket and stiff oval straw hat — the boater. Seldom could anyone relax sartorially like the three men with a boat (No. 133).

For shooting and for informal country occasions knickerbockers were much in evidence (Nos. 114, 115, 154). The Norfolk suit increased steadily in favour, being worn for cycling after about 1888. Previously, men wore either a lounge jacket or a 'patrol jacket' and tight knee-breeches (Nos. 117, 142). A variety of small cloth (No. 115) or felt country caps and hats were in use, and for several decades a square-crowned hard hat (No. 166) and a forerunner of the Homburg (No. 101). A high beehive-crowned bowler, sometimes of light colour (No. 160) was worn with the lounge suit. For town wear the eternal top hat—which was lower in the second half of the 'sixties, then shot up again ten years later (though never again to the height of the 'forties)— continued to offend the susceptibilities of artistic natures. 'Our tubular hats', sighed Charles Blanc, 'which artists in their everyday discourses have cast such withering scorn upon — these hats without front or back, without direction, without a culminating point, and whose frightful cylindrical shape is altogether

[1] C. W. & P. Cunnington, *Handbook of English Costume in the Nineteenth Century*, 1959.

at variance with the spherical form of the head, are assuredly the last remnant of barbarism.'[1]

From the 'eighties onward most young men wore a moustache, which remained general until the Great War (Nos. 141, 142, 145, 154, 234, 235) and some also had a Vandyke beard. The hair was worn uncurled and usually parted down the middle of the back as well as the front, until a side parting gradually began to come into fashion in the 'nineties. Old men often wore a full beard or retained the sidewhiskers of their youth (No. 228, 231).

In January 1888 at a private view at the Grosvenor Gallery, centre of the aesthetic movement, fashionable people noted with relief: 'The aesthetes had vanished; no more did dishevelled locks and crushed hats, balloon sleeves and weird ornaments proclaim the rebellion that raged against the dominion of Fashion in the realm of chiffons. The costumes of the ladies were neither eccentric nor particularly stylish.'[2]

During this year Directoire costumes and bonnets with wide brims flaring upward in front were made fashionable by Sarah Bernhardt in Victorien Sardou's drama 'La Tosca'. Bernhardt's stage costumes were not exact copies, but they influenced fashion by increasing the simplicity and decreasing the width of the skirt. The necessary corollary of a high waist was not accepted but only indicated by a sash or band of embroidery, and the skimpiness of the skirt was a matter of relativity, as it had been in the Empire revival of 1867. In the late 'eighties the Directoire and Empire style did not really catch on, but probably led to earlier abandonment of the tournure than would otherwise have been the case. 'Worth now eschews even the semblance of a bustle. The news seems almost too good to be true. We will actually be able to lean back in a carriage or on a chair once more.'[3] Nevertheless Princess Louise of Wales, who had recently married the Duke of Fife, still had her country clothes for Scotland made to go over a small bustle in autumn 1889 (No. 157). If the abandonment of the bustle were hailed with delight by the rational dress enthusiasts, it was regretted by other women for reasons that appear strange in our period when a figure like a pole is the ideal. 'No more corsets or tournures lending the simulated grace of curves to figures lacking the fullness of rounded outlines.'[4] In spring 1889 Parisians were shocked by the vogue that set in for plain skirts: 'such straight lines, such scanty use of draperies.'[5] In England this trend was welcomed as 'the age when simplicity reigns supreme. All superfluous ornaments are dispensed with'.''

[1] Charles Blanc, *Art and Ornament in Dress*, 1877.
[2] *The Queen*, Jan. 1888.
[3] *The Rational Dress Society's Gazette*, Sept. 1888.
[4] *The Woman's World*, Oct. 1888.
[5] *The Queen*, Feb. 1889.

If dress were a trifle simpler, the difficulty of deciding what to wear had increased. 'Twenty years ago you needed a morning dress, a visiting dress, a low-necked dinner dress, and a ball gown, the number of these being decided by individual requirements. Now women dress for dinner in as many different ways as the meal is served. Low gowns, half-high gowns, or teagowns which are akin to dressing-gowns, or teagowns that closely resemble the revised Court bodice, inspired by the modes of mediaeval times — all these are popular, and you have to know the habits of your host and hostess when you pack your trunks for a round of visits.'[1]

Just as Englishwomen had been slow in discarding the crinoline, they were reluctant to abandon the bustle. It was not until the beginning of 1890 that it could truly be said : 'Steels have disappeared, and pads are "beautifully less".'[2] In the winter expensive fur jackets were still made with a slit at the back in case the tournure were revived, as it had been once before. There was apparently still a deep-rooted desire for a bulge somewhere, and no sooner had it disappeared behind, than it began to grow on the upper arm.

The 'nineties began with sleeves slightly full, and set in with a little peak on the shoulder seam, which had started in 1889. Some had fullness from shoulder to elbow, of equal width from top to bottom. On evening dresses bows or feathers or gatherings sprouted upwards from the shoulder (No. 171). In 1892 the upper part of the sleeve began to grow in earnest (Nos. 172, 173) though it remained tight from elbow to wrist for the rest of the century. Expanding each season, in 1895–96 sleeves attained the maximum size conceivable (Nos. 174, 182, 183), so that the ultra-fashionable had to sidle through doors like a crab. These balloon sleeves were often made of different material from the rest of the dress; in 1892, for instance, enormous velvet sleeves in bright contrasting colours were a feature of evening gowns. The following year a large lace flounce round the neck stood out over the sleeves (No. 174). Lace had become high fashion again after a period of neglect during which fringe and jet had been preferred as trimming. In 1896 the leg-of-mutton or gigot sleeve appeared. This sleeve was narrow from the wrist to well above the elbow, and then expanded into soft folds, forming a puff. The enormous balloon sleeve continued to be worn alongside the new sleeve during that year.

Following the disappearance of the bustle, skirts were for a time comparatively narrow, falling smoothly without folds (No. 173). For walking they cleared the ground, revealing long pointed-toed button boots or shoes, and black stockings. For full evening dress the skirt extended into a train, and the stockings were white. Skirts opening down the front over an under-

[1] *The Woman's World*, Oct./Nov. 1889.   [2] *The Queen*, 1890.

skirt survived to a certain extent on dressy clothes, but from 1891 onward single skirts were more usual. They were comparatively plain — a novelty after so many decades of flounces, double skirts, and drapings. As sleeves widened, the skirt kept them company, and fears were expressed that the crinoline might return. Close-fitting at waist and hips, the skirt increased by means of goring to a wide hem-line, and had more fullness at the back than had recently been worn. The material was always solid and did not cling: brocade or satin in the evening, perhaps covered with lace (No. 172), stiff silk or cloth for day dresses. Paris declared eight yards the correct circumference at the hem; in London, where fashion was always less exaggerated, $5\frac{1}{2}$ yards was considered ample.[1] Either dimension would seem, from the evidence of photographs, to be an over-estimate. With the wide skirt and sleeves, it almost seemed that fashion was going back to 1830 for inspiration, yet in spite of a certain similarity, the dresses of the 'nineties were very different in spirit, being dignified rather than dashing, partly on account of the longer skirt.

The gored skirt being simple in appearance — though not in construction — particular attention was now paid to the upper part of the dress, which was more ornate. In 1890 the long-waisted bodice often had a cross-over front. Then came lace frills or jabots cascading down the front of the high-collared bodice. In 1893 'pelerine lapels' or big cape revers were revived for some years, and epaulettes added to the broad-shouldered effect.

The tailor-made was now in the familiar form of the coat and skirt, worn with a blouse, dear to Englishwomen off and on until quite recent years, and sure to be rehabilitated sooner or later. The same applies to the straw sailor hat, which appeared in the 1860s and never disappears for long. The coat and skirt of the 'nineties had a threequarter-length jacket with wide revers and of course big sleeves, and often a waistcoat (No. 170, 177). Blouses could be bought ready-made in great variety, to the disgust of dressmakers. They were also worn in their own right with a plain skirt, and there were dressy blouses for informal evening occasions. All had full sleeves, and the shirt-blouse for wearing with a suit had a starched collar, worn with a manly tie (No. 177, 178). A friend of my mother's, despairing at the limpness of her collars in India, had the idea of keeping them erect with circles of metal cut from food cans!

Cloaks and capes were more comfortable than a coat or mantle, as it was difficult to put on a sleeved outer garment even with the aid of sleeve-tongs. Many capes had a small Medici collar. Such upstanding collars were worn on evening dresses, 1888–92 (No. 172), and fur Medici collars on coats and jackets during the winter of 1889–90.

[1] *The Queen*, 1893.

Curves and Verticals

The bold lines of the skirt and sleeves found a counterpart in vivid colour schemes. Bright colours and strong contrasts were popular. Heliotrope and other shades of purple were fashionable, and yellow — often out of favour for long periods — was worn again. To me, yellow is a happy colour like sunshine, but it is supposed to symbolize envy and cowardice, and in intolerant periods expressed a stigma: Jews, lepers, and prisoners having been forced to wear it.

Apart from tailor-mades of tweed and other woollen cloth, less wool was worn than in the 'eighties; silk came back into favour for day dresses, and petticoats were intended to give an intriguing rustling sound. 'What would our grandmothers have thought of these extravagant tastes? The brocades, the glacé silks, and the satins used for petticoats are almost as elaborate as our dresses.'[1]

Except on the most formal occasions, bonnets were now seldom worn except by the elderly. Hats were of small or moderate size, often with a straight brim, and vertical trimming and nearly always perched rather high and straight on the head (Nos. 166–8, 170, 178). In the neo-Greek coiffure, the hair was dressed in a bunch or curls or a twist at the back, and with curls on the forehead (No. 181). Diamond stars, crescents and aigrettes were worn with evening dress (Nos. 171, 172, 174).

Among the well-known people who died in 1894 was Mrs. Amelia Jenks Bloomer of Seneca Falls, N.Y., who in 1849 had devised the first rational costume with Turkish-style trousers, tied in at the ankle. The bloomer costume did not catch on then, but a year after its designer's death, bloomers in the form of knickerbockers extending to below the knee and 'so full that they lack all indecorous suggestion' became a popular cycling costume for women. The old 'roadsters', which we call 'penny-farthings' were too high for any woman, however emancipated, but now there were 'dwarf bicycles' with two wheels of equal size. It was five years after smart Parisians had started cycling in the Bois de Boulogne that this sport became a craze among English society people, who went by carriage to Battersea Park to cycle. The more emancipated wore bloomers, the conventional preferred special skirts which could be buttoned round each leg in the form of a rational garment — the polite term for trousers — when on the machine. Other skirts could be turned up all round and fastened. The fact that an ordinary skirt, if full enough, was perfectly practicable (No. 170) was overlooked by most people. Nearly every tailor invented a bicycle skirt which he promptly patented. There was also the 'new patent fringe for cycling, with automatic fastening'. The curls were attached to a net, with two small combs to fix it to the real hair.

[1] *The Queen*, 1899.

178 *The Archduchess Stephanie, widow of Rudolph von Habsburg, by Alice Hughes, London, c. 1895*

177 *Mrs. Weir, by F. Hoeffler, Davos, c. 1899*

180   *The Princess of Wales at Mar Lodge, by W. & D. Downey, 1894*

179   *The Ladies Alexandra and Maud Duff, by Alice Hughes, London, 1895*

182   *The Duchess of Connaught, by Alice Hughes, London, 1895*

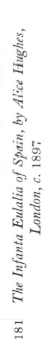

181   *The Infanta Eulalia of Spain, by Alice Hughes, London, c. 1897*

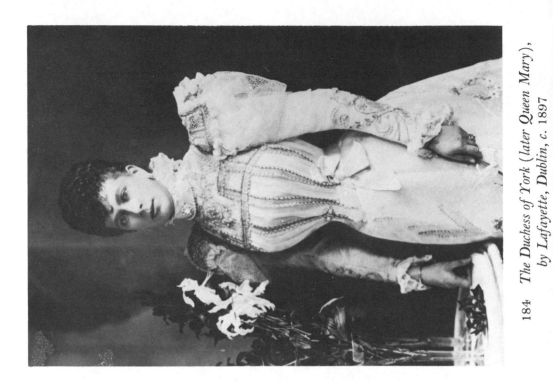

184 *The Duchess of York (later Queen Mary),
by Lafayette, Dublin, c. 1897*

183 *The Princess of Wales, Princess Maud of Wales and
her fiancé Prince Charles of Denmark. By W. & D. Downey,*

186   *Mr. and Mrs. Frederick MacMillan and friends, August 1901*

185   *(Sir) Austen Chamberlain, c. 1900*

187, 188 *Clothes for the seaside, 1901–2*

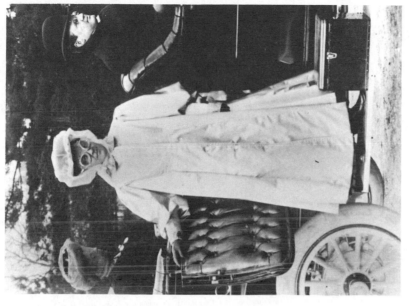

190   *Dust-coat and goggles, c. 1905*

189   *The Lady is going for a quiet drive with her chauffeur.*
April 1902

191   *Women playing hockey, by W. & H. Manor, c.* 1900

192   *Queenie and Gertrude play billiards, c.* 1903

193   *Visitors arriving at Henley station for the Regatta, c.* 1904

194   *Balloon race at Ranelagh, July* 1906

196 *Vera Blackhall, June 1905*

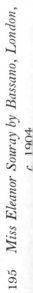

195 *Miss Eleanor Souray by Bassano, London,*
c. 1904

198 *The Archduchess Stephanie, by Alice Hughes.*
London, c. 1905

197 *Miss Camille Clifford, the personification of*
the Gibson Girl, c. 1906

199 *A lady, by H. Walter Barnett, London, c. 1906*

200 *A lady, by Armand Daudoy, Namurs, c. 1903*

201 Queen Alexandra with her daughters at Windsor Castle,
15 June 1905

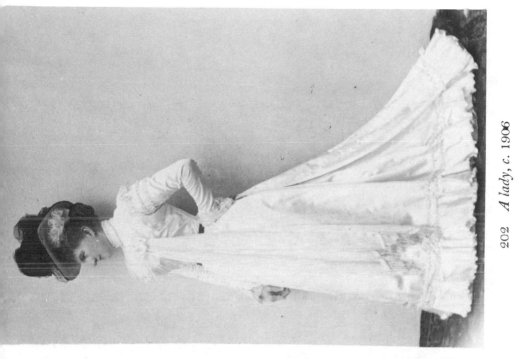

202 A lady, c. 1906

203 *Group of Austrian Archdukes and Archduchesses, c. 1906*

204 *Balloon race at Ranelagh, by Arthur Barrett, 1908*

205　Miss Lily Elsie as 'The Merry Widow'.

206　Miss Marie George, by Bassano, London, c.1911

208 *Mrs. Brown Potter, by Foulsham & Banfield, London, c. 1909*

207 *Colossal hat, c. 1910*

210 *Miss Pauline Chase, by Reutlinger, Paris, c. 1910*

209 *Mrs. Charles A. Wilson, Aberdeen, 1909*

212   *Members of the Women's Freedom League of non-militant suffragists, c. 1911*

211   *Sir George and Lady Alexander in Paris, c. 1910*

213   '*Black Ascot*', 1910

214   *Lady Ormonde and Lady Constance Butler at Cowes, August* 1910

215   *Marriage of the Archduke Karl to*
Princess Zita of Bourbon and Parma, 21 October 1911

216   *Yeomanry sports at Blenheim Palace, May* 1911

218 *Trouser-skirt which caused a sensation at the Auteuil races,*

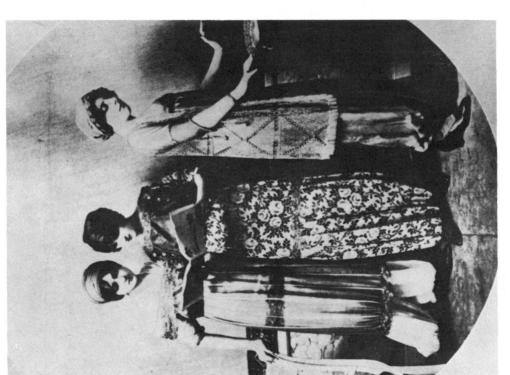

217 *Dresses and turbans designed by Paul Poiret, March 1911*

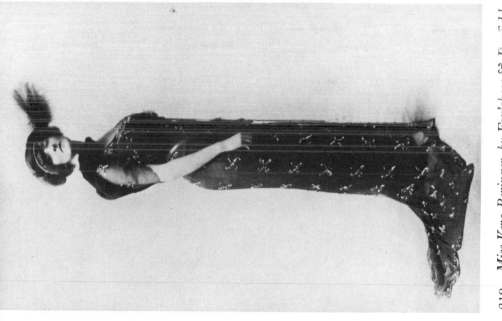

219   *Miss Vera Beringer, by Foulsham & Banfield, London, c. 1911*

220   *A startling fashion at Auteuil races, July 1912*

221   *The new ballroom at the Hyde Park Hotel, by E. Walter Barnett, 1912*

*Miss Baden-Powell, Chief of the Girl Guides,
by Mrs. Broom, c. 1913*

225

222 *Ascot, 1913*

224   *Fair in aid of Our Dumb Friends League*, 20 *June* 1913

225   *Ascot*, 1914

226   *Mr. and Mrs. Winston Churchill at the Hendon air pageant, 1914*

228 *John Tyndall, by Herbert Barraud, 1888.*

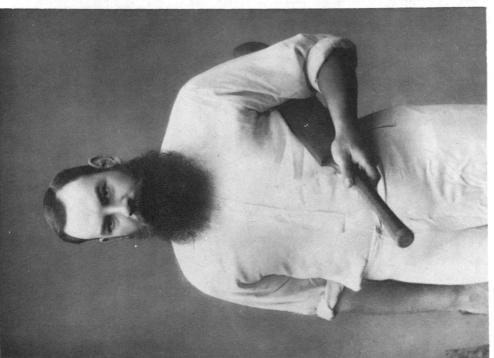

227 *W. G. Grace, by Herbert Barraud, 1887. Full beard*

229 *Hans von Bülow, by E. Bieber, Berlin, c. 1890.*
Goatee beard

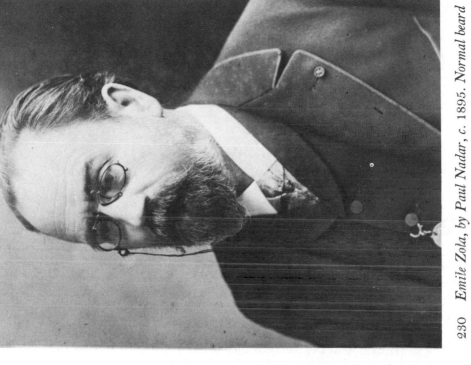

230 *Emile Zola, by Paul Nadar, c. 1895. Normal beard*

231 *Thomas H. Huxley, by A. G. Dew Smith, c. 1885.*

232 *An old gentleman with sidewhiskers, c. 1857*

234 *Kaiser Wilhelm II, 1889. 'Kaiser moustache'.*

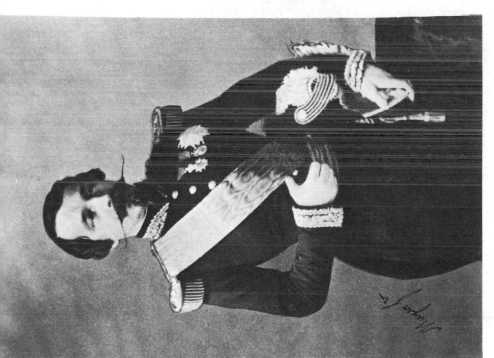

233 *Napoleon III, by Mayer frères, 1854.*
Long waxed moustache

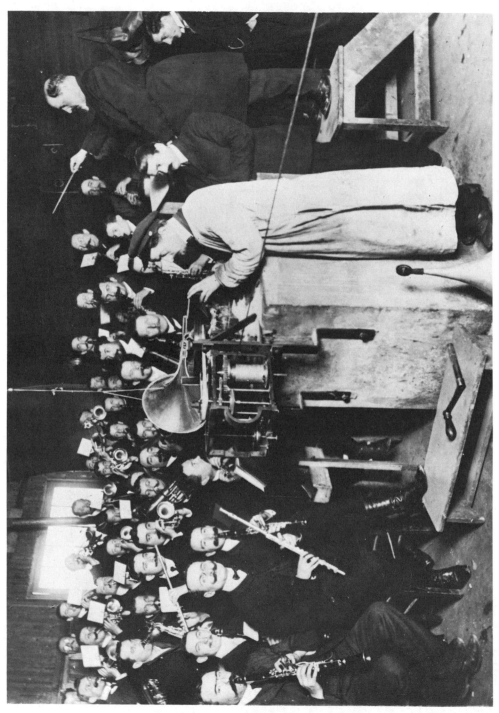

235　A French orchestra at a gramophone recording session, c. 1905

Curves and Verticals

During the winter of 1895–96 Battersea Park was neglected for Hyde Park, where society people rode their bicycles during the permitted hours from nine to twelve, between the Achilles statue and the powder magazine. 'Many of the ladies carry very large muffs, putting both hands in at once — a somewhat dangerous practice.'[1] On fine mornings two to three thousand cyclists pedalled up and down. Many of them being débutantes, the necessity for a cycling chaperon was discussed, and 'it is said that more than one lady who is mistress of the art has announced herself ready to undertake the duties. If young ladies are to be allowed to pedal themselves about in so public a place as London, then it will be necessary to provide them with some proper escort, since it would be adding rather too cruelly to the burden of a society mother's day's work, had she to accompany her daughters on their matutinal wheeling expeditions.'[2]

In 1899 Viscountess Harberton, cycling in her rational costume, asked for refreshment at the Hautboy Hotel in Ockham, but the landlady refused to let her go into the public coffee room, offering instead to serve her in the bar parlour. Lady Harberton, in defence of emancipated dress, took her to court, but the jury decided that the bar parlour was 'a decent and proper place' and returned a verdict of Not Guilty. By this time, bicycling was no longer a fashionable sport, having been taken up by the middle and lower classes (No. 175) as a means of transport — a factor which helped to expedite the growing freedom gradually being accorded to young women. But it was a good many years before old-fashioned people could get used to the sight of unchaperoned girl cyclists in bloomers, as can be seen from a letter quoted by Mrs. C. S. Peel. 'Two ladies — or, as Grandpapa says, two shameless females — in bloomers bicycled through the village yesterday, and some of the women were so scandalized that they threw stones at them. I didn't dare to say so, but I thought they looked very neat, though I don't think I should quite like to show my own legs to the world like that.'[3] Concluding her letter, the writer raised the problem of every generation: 'Why do old people always disapprove of anything which they didn't do when they were young?'

Another thing old people found shocking was make-up, which was discreetly applied by a few go-ahead women. Hardly any were bold enough to put on make-up openly before the 1920s. A surreptitious wipe-over with a leaf of *papier poudré* torn from a little purple book was all most women dared to do. In 1905 the little girl in No. 196, appearing in this dress in a charity performance of *tableaux vivants* before King Edward VII, was shocked to see ladies being made up for the stage, and when her turn came burst into tears, crying: 'I don't want to be painted like Jesebel and go to Hell!' Sir Max Beerbohm

[1] *The Queen*, Jan. 1896.   [2] ibid.   [3] Mrs. C. S. Peel, *A Hundred Wonderful Years*, 1926.

81

revealed in his essay 'A Defence of Cosmetics' that the use of make-up was becoming general in the 'nineties, and 'most women are not as young as they are painted'.[1] In his approval and, indeed, recommendation, Beerbohm went further than Mrs. Haweis dared fifteen years earlier. 'Cosmetics are not going to be a mere prosaic remedy for age or plainness, but all ladies and girls will come to love them. . . . The season of the unsophisticated is gone by, and the young girl's final extinction beneath the rising tides of cosmetics will leave no gap in life and will rob art of nothing. . . . Artifice, sweetest exile, is come into her kingdom.'[2] Sun-tan make-up was used by 'countless gentlemen who walk about town in the time of its desertion from August to October, artificially bronzed, as though they were fresh from the moors or from the Solent. This, I conceive, is done for purely social reasons.'[3]

The frock coat in grey as well as black had made a come-back just before 1890, knee length and close-fitting, with silk-faced lapels (No. 164), and for a few years longer held its position as 'the supreme exponent of fashion' for afternoon wear in town, and on all solemn occasions. An old dandy whom Beerbohm jokingly asked what he would wear on the Day of Judgment replied gravely : 'If I had been a saint I should certainly wear a light suit, with a white waistcoat and a flower, but I am no saint. I shall probably wear black trousers or trousers of some very dark blue, and a frock-coat, tightly buttoned.' The frock coat was already doomed by the domination of the morning coat, and that in turn by the lounge suit, which in the closing years of the nineteenth century began to be worn even in the West End in the morning. With the lounge suit a soft-fronted coloured shirt became for the first time permissible, though the collar had to be white and stiff. The bow tie or the ordinary long tie were worn, and as headgear either a bowler hat or the modern type of felt or Homburg hat popularized by the Prince of Wales (later Edward VII) after his first stay in that spa in 1889. A hat on the lines of the Homburg had been worn before this, however (No. 101). Another fashion in men's wear that came in during the 'nineties was the vertical crease down the front and back of the trousers. From 1896 onward the trousers of lounge suits, but not of formal suits, began to be worn turned up.

'Fashions that will come after, can never improve upon those which are ushering in the first summer of the new century.'[4] This confident assertion is typical of most fashion journalists' uncritical acceptance of each new style as the most attractive ever. It does, perhaps, come closer than usual to justification in describing the graceful *art nouveau* gowns with their long convolvulus-like curves, trailing boas and trains.

[1] *The Yellow Book*, April 1894.   [2] ibid.   [3] ibid.   [4] *The Queen*, 1901.

For nearly ten years women's clothes were homogeneous in their principal lines, apart from variations in detail and decoration. The new style had already been heralded in the year of Queen Victoria's Diamond Jubilee. The wonderful 'Queen's Weather' on which the sovereign could almost rely, encouraged the use of thin fabrics such as muslin, gauze, chiffon and lace, and stiffness of outline disappeared through the abandonment of heavy materials, except for tailor-mades. Before the Queen's death, most of the main features we associate with the clothes and attitudes of Edward VII's reign had already begun to make their appearance.

In the early Edwardian period graceful clinging gowns covered a new swan-like figure achieved by a long straight-fronted corset which forced the body into a pronounced S-bend. The bosom, encased if necessary in a 'Neena' bust improver 'modelled from the Venus de Milo', was thrust forward, and balanced by 'the hips at the back', as the posterior was delicately termed. The high stance of the chin completed the majestic, self-confident and indeed rather self-satisfied attitude of the 'Gibson girl' — an ideal type created by the American artist Charles Dana Gibson in 1901, inspired by his wife, and personified on the London stage by Camille Clifford (No. 197) in *The Belle of Mayfair*. In her, fashion's ideal figure was achieved in reality, although the complete lack of applied decoration on her dress is uncharacteristic.

Accustomed as we are to tight skirts we can hardly appreciate the novelty of fitted hips to the Edwardians: 'One thing is certain, the skirt must fit like wax at the top, and fall in full, graceful folds at the foot'[1] with a flare achieved either by goring or by the addition of a flounce. Afternoon as well as evening dresses had a train, and when standing this was often pulled forward in a swirling spiral (Nos. 197, 199, 201). Basically, this type of skirt was worn from 1897 to 1907, and being less full than the 'nineties skirt, it was difficult to hold up when walking.

To reduce the apparent size of the waist by contrast, pads were sometimes worn on the hips and at the sides of the chest. The whole figure was a system of curves. Boleros — close-fitting coatees with a curved edge, something on the lines of the Zouave jacket but much smaller, were a feature of many day bodices (No. 186). Owing to the great popularity of blouses, bodices were all pouched and pulled down to below the waistline in front, which was considered to give 'a graceful length to the figure'. This characteristic early Edwardian 'kangaroo pouch' (Nos. 193–5, 200, 201) — a small artistic flaw in *art nouveau* dress — was in fashion from 1898 to 1905 and still appeared on some later dresses. Until 1913 the neck was covered in the daytime by a high tight collar

[1] *The Queen*, 1899.

of net or lace stiffened with vertical strips of whalebone, celluloid, or wire; and often by a jewelled 'dog collar' (Nos. 198, 201) in the evening or even day. 'For those who dress their hair high and adopt the present vogue for flat shoulders to the sleeves, something fussy round the neck is absolutely necessary.'[1] This was the long stole or boa of ruffled chiffon, or of ostrich feathers sometimes costing as much as ten guineas, so characteristic of the period (Nos. 194, 200, 201).

The full sleeve subsided in 1897 into a vestigial puff or epaulette which disappeared within two years, leaving a long tight sleeve extending in a point over the hand. Evening sleeves were mere draperies of lace. With the new century, elaboration of the sleeve after a short interim period of plain tight ones began again, the fullness now being between elbow and wrist on dresses, though Edwardian tailor-mades often had the sleeves set in with fullness at the shoulder. Pagoda sleeves with a white *engageante*, similar to though much narrower than those worn half a century earlier, reappeared, and other designs expanded into a pouch, or into frills. In 1904–6 there were even some sleeves again full between shoulder and elbow, but now limp instead of stiff like those of ten years earlier, and not nearly so big.

The new habit of society people of spending the late winter and spring on the Côte d'Azur led to a special type of dressy day gown for visiting the casino at Monte Carlo, where a hat or toque — a stringless bonnet — was often worn even with evening gowns. 'At Monte Carlo the toque rules, and to be a self-respecting toque it must present a squashed appearance'.[2] Some toques were made entirely of artificial flowers.

London clothes were now so elegant that it was said 'the visiting toilet no longer exists. We can pay calls without being got up specially for the occasion.'[3] In the last year of the nineteenth century lace was the dominant feature — and remained so for several years. Without lace, no dress was complete, and all the best of the evening gowns were entirely made of lace. Many women possessed valuable antique lace which they re-furbished again and again to trim their dresses, petticoats, and sunshades. Lace even appeared as an incongruous decoration on fur coats. Conversely, lace dresses were trimmed with fur (No. 181). Such combinations seem perverse and in bad taste.

In the early twentieth century white was more worn than at any time since the days of Napoleon I, even by middle-aged women. These were the great days of the mature beauty (No. 198, 201). In the summer, lingerie hats were worn by children (No. 196) and grown-ups (No. 193) alike.

'There has probably never been a season when fashions were more charming

[1] *The Lady*, 1903. [2] *The Queen*, 1898. [3] ibid.

or more elaborate', it was said at the time of Edward VII's coronation. 'Not only are the fabrics of exquisite texture, but they are embellished with miraculously fine hand-embroidery, appliqué lace insertions, trimming of many kinds; and the success of a gown or wrap really depends on the style and originality of the trimming more than on any other point.'[1] As the line had changed very little in the last five years, fashion concentrated on trimmings. 'Ball gowns of soft textures are much tucked and inlet with insertion and medallions of lace, and flounces or frills surround the hem. The appliqué craze has reached such a height that even flowers and artificial foliage are now arranged in this fashion. Garnitures of pearls, groups of tinsel butterflies or dragonflies, and *choux* of velvet or satin, edged with pearly or coral beads, are favourite adornments. White lace robes are encrusted with appliqués of black lace, and black lace robes with the heavier type of Venice point in cream or écru.'[2]

Expensive through the vast amount of handwork that went into them, producing an effect of massive daintiness, Edwardian dresses, though sumptuous, were seldom showy in spite of the abundance of embroidery, sequins, 'bugles', and lace, for colours were pale and delicate. 'It is characteristic of the English nation to shun colours', declared Mrs. Eric Pritchard,[3] a friend of Lady Warwick, rather sweepingly. Mrs. Merrifield and Hippolyte Taine had expressed the opposite opinion. Fashion alternates between bright and neutral colours, which are seldom equally in favour. When fashion demands subtle hues, bright colours look vulgar, but when vivid colours are 'in' only dowdy people wear 'safe' neutral tints.

Much of the extravagance of Edwardian dress lay beneath the surface. This was above all the era of seductive underclothes, when a model petticoat might cost as much as £50. 'Exquisite lingerie forms the foundation of the wardrobe of the woman of refinement' decreed Mrs. Pritchard.[4] She advised women with a dress allowance of 'only' £200 a year (equal to £1000 today) to put aside one-fifth for lingerie and corsets, 'for the Cult of Chiffon has this in common with the Christian religion — it insists that the invisible is more important than the visible.' Her objection to women wearing hideous woollen or flannel undergarments is not difficult to fathom: 'Can one wonder that marriage is so often a failure, and that the English husband of such a class of woman goes where he can admire the petticoat of aspirations?' By this she meant lace-trimmed petticoats made of satin, brocade, or silk in blue, pink, yellow, or even black — 'wonderfully becoming to a fair woman'. By 1902 it had become unsubtle, even vulgar, for petticoats to be audible. 'When I hear the rustling of

[1] *The Lady*, 1902.   [2] *The Lady*, 1902.   [3] Mrs. Eric Pritchard, *The Cult of Chiffon*, 1902.
[4] ibid.

an expensive silk petticoat, I should like to shout for the police.' Stiff glacé silk and taffetas were therefore a thing of the past — at any rate for the petticoat of aspirations. Suburban women, on the other hand (or their husbands?) still liked the rustling sound of the 'Invincible' Skirt sold by Stagg & Mantle at 8s. 6d., and its gaudy colours. 'The above Underskirt is made of Bright Moreen, with three frills of Glacé Silk forming flounces, and is confidently recommended for its excellent shape, durability and smart effect. Colours : Cardinal, violet, scarlet, mauve, pink, sky, navy, heliotrope, cerise, fawn and black.'[1]

Anyone less well off than Mrs. Pritchard's circle of friends could certainly dress nicely on a fraction of the amount mentioned by her. A coat and skirt could be made to order in Mayfair for $4\frac{1}{2}$ to $5\frac{1}{2}$ guineas, copies of French model dresses were obtainable at D. H. Evans for 12 guineas, and beautiful teagowns for £5 at Dickens & Jones. In a half-price sale, the Wholesale Fur Company offered mink jackets for ten guineas. Court shoes of kid with long pointed toes and Louis heels cost 5s. 11d. to 8s. 11d. at the London Shoe Company in New Bond Street; silk stockings 1s. 11d., long white kid 20-button evening gloves 5s. 11d., 16-button suede for day wear in shades of beige, putty, mocha, and light grey were only 1s. 11d. White kid was essential for 'smart toilettes' worn, for instance, at an At Home. In order to indicate that the call would be a short one, the parasol was taken into the drawing room and the gloves were not removed for tea. Thin bread and butter was rolled into cylinders, with the butter inside; if something stickier were offered, the fingers of one hand were carefully withdrawn from the glove, leaving it buttoned on the arm. This was no easy feat, for gloves were so tight that 'twenty minutes should be allowed for fitting on a new pair'. The fastidious Mrs. Pritchard laid down that 'a really well-dressed woman has her gloves made for her with as great care as her boots, although nowadays we can get the best makes and be almost perfectly fitted'.

It was reckoned in 1902 that a society woman obliged to economize could manage on £50 for her clothes for the London season, provided she did not aspire to models from Worth or Paquin, which cost up to £200. The following table[2] sets out the items considered necessary in those days on an economy budget. As against three pairs of shoes, 18 pairs of gloves strike one nowadays as excessive for a three months' period — until one remembers the At Homes!

Hairdresser	£2 10s. including alterations or additions to *toupée*
Millinery	£3 10s. three toques or hats

---

[1] Advertisement in *The Lady*, 1902.   [2] *The Lady*, 1902.

Boots and shoes	£2 10s.	1 pr. smart walking shoes, 1 pr. boots, 1 pr. evening shoes
Gloves	£1 10s.	10 prs. suede, 6 pr. kid, 2 pr. long evening gloves.
Mantles and ruffles	£6 10s.	
Petticoats and hosiery	£2 5s.	
Parasols (2)	£1 16s.	
Gowns, blouses, etc.	£25	
Odds and ends	£4 9s.	

The first item in the list is significant. It was essential to have a very full head of hair, and *toupées* or 'transformations' amounting to complete wigs were worn by quite young women. Not since the abandonment of the chignon in the mid-'seventies had extra hair been so unselfconsciously added. The hair—often reddened with henna — was dressed full and high, with the front part raised over a 'rat' in so-called Pompadour style (No. 197, left 201) — a modest emulation of the towering head-dresses of the 1770s, which the Marquise did not live to see. The hair was waved with hot tongs in the technique devised by the Parisian hairdresser Marcel in the 'nineties. 'Most women have learned by sad experience that it simply ruins their own hair to have it waved even two or three times in the course of a week; but with one of these nice transformations [price 12 guineas] all such trouble is avoided, and the length of time occupied by one's toilette shortened in a quite wonderful manner '[1] In 1906 Charles Nestlé introduced permanent waving — a major operation lasting eight to twelve hours, and costing £250.[2] Other modern forms of beauty culture were beginning to be introduced: electrolysis for removing superfluous hair, chin-straps to cure double chins, and 'Trilene tablets to reduce weight and cure corpulency without change of diet'.

The bonnet as a fashion article had died with the nineteenth century. The variety of Edwardian hats was great, their common feature being lavish trimming, especially ostrich feathers. Only the toque dispensed with a brim, and was especially favoured by Queen Alexandra and the Princess of Wales (later Queen Mary) as it did not screen their faces from the public. One can hardly think of either of these royal ladies without a toque, but of course this does not apply to their earlier years.

During the first decade of the twentieth century a new dress reform movement started in Germany, advocating a shapeless garment worn without a corset, which was, of course, anathema to fashionable people. 'Reformed dress

[1] ibid.   [2] Ruth Turner Wilcox, *The Mode in Hats and Head Dress*, 1945.

is above all hygienic', explains the wearer of a sack-like dress and broad sandals to a *chic* acquaintance, 'and keeps the body fit for the functions of motherhood.' 'As long as you wear that rag, you're hardly likely to get into that condition' was the tart reply.[1]

The Edwardians liked to dress up on every possible occasion. Until the First World War, women had far more leisure and opportunities to parade in finery in the daytime than they have, or wish for, nowadays. Clothes were more of a status symbol than today when the majority of people can afford to dress well. Exquisite gowns were to be seen at garden parties, the races (not only Ascot), flower shows, Ranelagh, fêtes of all kinds, and regattas. At Henley women wore frilly dresses and hats (No. 193) whereas men were more casually dressed (apart from the stiff collar) in blazers and white trousers — sometimes with black shoes — and the inevitable 'boater' (No. 193). A good deal of this dressing up was no doubt due to vanity and pretentiousness, yet the wish to wear something more alluring than a black leather jacket and jeans does seem in keeping with natural feminine instinct. Beatniks have created a style of their own as part of an anti-bourgeois revolt. Their attitude is in some ways not unlike that of the Bohemians of the Latin Quarter in the 1840s, only they were men, and their women dressed as well as they could afford.

In striking contrast to Edwardian feminine frills was the tailored coat and skirt (Nos. 192, 209) now a classic for the country, sport, travel, and even morning wear in town. Navy blue or cream-coloured serge was much worn in summer, and face-cloth in winter. For active use the skirt might be only ankle length. Stockings were black or dark brown, and with this outfit went sensible laced Oxford shoes or long buttoned boots, and a shirt-blouse with manly collar and cuffs. In summer a stiff straw sailor hat completed the ensemble, at other seasons a felt hat on the lines of a man's Homburg: this refers to the early Edwardian period; at the end of the reign big hats were often worn even with plain tailor-mades (Nos. 210, 212, 214). This tailored style of dressing was favoured by women who had a job, and by many a suffragette. For middle-class and the less affluent society women, a tailor-made suit was a great stand-by, and remained so until quite recent years. Indeed, as mass-production of dresses and coats became more widespread, the conventional made-to-measure tailored suit of high quality material, cut, fit, and finish, gained in prestige until eventually it induced in the wearer a kind of anti-fashion feeling of superiority which did not quite disappear even when the suit was old and out of date. 'A tailor-made suit always looks good!' was the motto of countless English-women up to about 1950, relying on the fact that everyone who mattered could

[1] *Simplicissimus*, Berlin, 1909.

see that it was expensive. This thought consoled those who could not afford to be in the forefront of fashion.

After the repeal of the 'Red Flag' Act in 1896, motoring became an exceedingly fashionable pastime, and was by many people considered a healthy exercise. 'The easy jolting which occurs when a motor-car is driven at a fair speed over the highway conduces to a healthy agitation' wrote Sir Henry Thompson.[1] 'It "acts on the liver", to use a popular phrase, which means only that it aids the peristaltic movements of the bowels and promotes the performance of their functions. Horse-riding has, however, the advantage of necessitating exercise of the muscles of the legs. This is one of the disadvantages of motoring, but I have found that it may be to some extent overcome by alighting at the end of a drive of twenty miles, and running smartly for about two hundred or three hundred yards. I make this a practice in relation to my motor drives.'

Until the dusty roads had been macadamized or covered cars introduced, motorists needed special protective clothing when the 'horseless carriage' was taken out of the 'motor stable' for a drive. In 1902 — when the maximum speed of 'light locomotives' was still limited to 12 m.p.h. — Lady Jeune advised women what to wear in order to be warm and comfortable 'with as little disfigurement as possible'. In winter a warm dress and underclothes had to be worn under a top coat of waterproof material lined with chamois leather and fur, long and wide enough to wrap well round the legs. A grey Shetland veil two yards long and threequarters of a yard wide could be pulled right over the face if needed. In summer a gauze veil and a dustcoat were sufficient. The hardest concession a woman had to make, according to Lady Jeune, for motoring, was the need for goggles, necessary both for comfort and the preservation of the eyesight. 'They are not becoming, but appearance must be sacrificed if motor-driving is to be thoroughly enjoyed' (No. 190). 'Those who fear any detriment to their good looks had best content themselves with a quiet drive in the park'[2] (No. 189). A wide, round flat tweed or cloth cap worn by many women motorists was sometimes — though unbecoming — also sported on other occasions, to imply that the wearer belonged to the new motoring class (No. 192).

As for men, the President of the Automobile Club de France, Baron de Zuylen de Nyevelt, admitted that the clothes worn by many motorists had been 'the subject of much irreverent ribaldry. It is difficult to imagine anything more grotesque than the appearance of some whose enthusiasm makes them forgetful of their appearance.'[3] Conspicuousness could be avoided by wearing a

---

[1] *Motors and Motor-Driving*, ed. by Alfred C. Harmsworth, 2nd edition, 1902.
[2] ibid.   [3] ibid.

Norfolk suit cut in the ordinary way except that the sleeves buttoned tightly round the wrist. In winter the top-coat was lined with fur and had a high fur-lined collar. In summer a dust-coat was worn. 'Generally speaking, there appears no reason why, apart from the goggles, a motor owner cannot dress in such a manner as thoroughly to protect himself from cold and at the same time retain so ordinary an appearance as to avoid public attention.'

'Lady cyclists are or used to be a great danger', wrote another motorist of this period, 'for when a motor was heard approaching them from behind, they usually fell off their bicycles, apparently in terror; but this distressing spectacle is now comparatively seldom seen.'[1] A full 'short' skirt was now usual for cyclists, who had realized there was no need for a divided garment.

Despite street improvements and widened thoroughfares, the traffic problem in London was steadily increasing, but it was optimistically declared that when motor-cars replaced horse-drawn vehicles they would 'by taking up less space, relieve the streets of a considerable amount of pressure'.[2]

In the early twentieth century Saville Row tailors' charges were eight guineas for a morning suit and eleven guineas for evening clothes.[3] Yet if no single male garment approached the cost of a Paris model, the man of fashion nevertheless spent a great deal on large quantities of clothes. King Edward VII, Europe's *arbiter elegantiarum*, used to take forty suits and over twenty pairs of shoes on his Continental holidays. An innovator in dress, he had worn the bowler hat as an undergraduate in 1859, and thirty years later introduced the Homburg, which survives as the ordinary modern felt hat. He is also credited with the introduction of the trouser crease in 1860, trying it out sideways as well as back and front, but photographs only show a seam-line (No. 112) at the side. In fact, the Prince of Wales did not wear the crease until it came into general use in the 'nineties.

In spring 1907 the first stirrings of a fundamental change in women's fashions became evident. The waistline was slightly raised and less tight, the hips smaller, skirts less full, and 'the absence of frills and flounces of the ortho-dox "frilly" type quite conspicuous'.[4] Striped materials, which do not call for applied decoration, were much worn, and peplum skirts with tassels at the points. Lace still remained fashionable for races and garden parties. The following year skirts became narrower and hats larger. The hair was dressed wide in an attempt not to be eclipsed by the large-crowned hats laden with ostrich feathers, aigrets, birds of Paradise, or big flowers. These were the famous 'Merry Widow' hats worn by Lily Elsie in the first London production

[1] *Motors and Motor-Driving*, 2nd ed. 1902.   [2] *The Lady*, Aug. 1902.
[3] George Cornwallis-West, *Edwardian Hey-Days*, 1930.   [4] *The Lady*, April 1907.

of Léhar's operetta in 1908 (No. 205). The habit of wearing a hat with evening dress (frontispiece) in Continental casinos, restaurants and theatres had caught on in London, and naturally caused much annoyance in the auditorium. Some years earlier when hats were beginning to get larger, a man having his view obstructed requested a lady to remove her hat. 'I've paid ten shillings for my seat and I want to see the stage.' 'And I've paid ten guineas for my hat, and I want it to be seen' was the disconcerting reply.[1]

The *habillé* tailor-made was much worn in town for all informal occasions (No. 210). Some of those designed in Paris even had a small train to the straight and narrow skirt, and the jackets were three-quarter length, cut away in front below the waist. Buttons were very large; otherwise the suits were 'quite singularly simple and free of decoration'.

From 1909 onward enormous flat muffs (No. 207) replaced the small barrel muff. Astrakhan had fallen from favour because it had become too common. Sable retained its prestige, moleskin and the luxurious grey chinchilla were much worn in the late Edwardian period, and winter, 1909, saw the triumph of the unattractive skunk. The muff was usually held rather high and away from the body. The late Edwardian woman stood very erect. Slim vertical lines had triumphed over stately mature curves; corsets hardly went in at the waist.

At the beginning of George V's reign the hobble skirt made a tentative appearance in England. Already in March 1910 an Englishwoman visiting Paris wrote in astonishment of a dress she saw in which 'the material narrows the skirt to its hem, which is so scanty in width that it seems to tie in the feet! I must tell you there are no collars in the new dresses; the necks are all bare!' She also described 'a neat costume of apricot coloured cloth with a close-fitting skirt held with a bias band round the feet'.[2]

At 'Black Ascot' women in mourning for King Edward had by no means all taken to the new style. Conventional people clearly felt that a train was a necessary adjunct on a fashionable occasion (No. 213 left), but the bolder spirits wore narrow ground-length dresses with a long tunic over a skirt of less diameter than their hat, the brim being wider than ever, though the crown was a trifle less clumsy. In 1910 and 1911 the fashionable proportion was three to two : circumference of hat six feet, of hem four feet.

The exaggerated hobble skirt was a garment for the ultra-fashionable and probably found no more general acceptance than the almost equally hampering short tight skirts of 1958–61, judging from photographs rather than the drawings in fashion magazines. 'The hobble skirt, except in the most modified form, has not been countenanced by our social leaders', wrote *The Sphere* in

[1] *Punch*, 8 November 1899.   [2] *The Lady*, March 1910.

January 1911. Certainly it found no favour among royalty. It was never worn by Queen Mary, who disliked anything *outré*, and obviously it was impossible for women to curtsey in it. No. 221 shows the dresses worn at a Court in 1912, after the débutantes had laid aside their trains and feathers to dance at the Hyde Park Hotel. The happy wedding photograph of the heir-presumptive of Austria-Hungary in October 1911 (No. 215) shows dresses too wide to be fashionable.

Some evening dresses of this period come closer to the classical Empire gown in form, though not in material (No. 219) than any other revival of that recurring style. Others had overskirts of gauze or chiffon embroidered with beads or diamanté, or a draped effect round the feet, and for full dress, a tiny pointed train coming from the side or even front of the skirt — a degenerate wisp which had little in common with the sweeping dignity of former trains. The greatest novelty was the harem skirt which caused a sensation early in 1911. At least it provided a better answer to the problem how to take a step than the one given by a *Punch* cartoon[1] of two hobble-skirted young women hurrying at a station. 'You'll never catch the train if you keep on trying to *run*!' protests one of them, proceeding like a kangaroo by short leaps with both feet together.

As early as January 1911 *The Sphere* mentions the Turkish skirt designed by an unnamed French *couturier* — doubtless Paul Poiret. Before 1904 this *enfant terrible* of the Paris fashion world had infuriated his employer Jean Worth — son of the original Charles Frederick Worth — by designing a dress on simple vertical lines, instead of the ubiquitous curves. Having set up a *salon* of his own, Poiret developed his ideas independently, it seems, of Bakst's brilliant designs for the Russian ballet *Scheherezade* (1910). The hobble skirt, the harem trouser-skirt, vivid oriental colours in place of pastel shades, were among Poiret's contributions to fashion. Another was his influence towards the waistless corset and easy-fitting bodice. Nevertheless, it was harem skirts worn by mannequins of Drécoll and Béchoff-David, not Poiret, which astonished the crowds at the Auteuil races in March 1911 (No. 218). 'The courageous wearers were unmercifully chaffed by the crowd. . . . There seems little probability of it becoming a popular fashion in England.'[2]

The harem skirt or *jupe culotte* was sometimes a real divided skirt clearly separated at the knee, but for evening wear it consisted of baggy trousers half hidden under a tunic or overdress open at the sides (No. 217). Another design was less conspicuous : an instep-length narrow skirt slit up at the left side or in front was worn over trousers gathered in at the ankles, which were by no

[1] *Punch*, 20 April 1910.   [2] *The Sphere*, 11 March 1911.

means obtrusive (No. 218). However, the mere idea of trousers for women seemed utterly incongruous, and the attempted fashion died out as completely as the rational dress of the 'eighties had. I have never seen a photograph of a private individual wearing it, only reproductions of models in magazines. But the slit-up skirt remained, for after all even fashionable women had to be able to walk at least short distances, and to dance. The tango was just coming in, and it is with this dance that the dresses of the next few years — though entirely lacking Argentinian influence — are closely associated. In fact the slit skirt came to be called the tango skirt and with it were worn so-called 'cothurn' shoes (but with thin soles), with cross-over ribbons right up the leg, or Cleopatra sandals trimmed with a cameo. Buckled Cromwell shoes, and shoes with three straps over the instep, were also popular. Thin high-heeled shoes and transparent stockings, often matching the dress, were now worn out of doors in winter. Even women without a motor car or carriage abandoned the sensible buttoned boot, though there were still some boots of a lighter type, with a gaiter effect in a pale colour.

Small hats and toques began to rival the cartwheels which everyone was beginning to get tired of, though shady hats continued to be worn in summer until the late 1920s when for the first time in history a brown instead of a fair skin was found attractive in European women, being a visible proof of Mediterranean or winter sports holidays. The small hats of 1912–14 were mostly rather undistinguished round or oval shapes, trimmed with upstanding aigrettes or osprey feathers. In reaction to the exuberant curled ostrich plumes that had been in favour so long, the weedy, skimpy-looking and undecorative ospreys were *chic* for no other reason than that everyone knew how expensive they were (No. 225).

The desire to create a sensation at any price sometimes leads to the most incongruous stunts. Fashion designers and occasionally society women have been particularly prone to such extravaganza. In summer 1912 Lady Warwick carried with a light garden-party dress a big muff of thin white material trimmed with roses and two bands of fur. Not only was this a perverse juxtaposition, but even an English summer hardly calls for a muff, and one made of thin material is a contradiction in terms.[1]

The simple tubular skirt was soon elaborated by swathing the material round the legs, and in 1913–14 the addition of a tunic from waist to knee (No. 225) and scarves or sashes arranged vertically (No. 222) or horizontally (No. 226). Many women, however, refrained from such fantasies, and Nos. 224, 225 are typical of what well-dressed but not ultra-fashionable women were wearing.

[1] *Les Modes*, 1912.

Curves and Verticals

Around 1913 dresses became 'low-necked' in comparison with the high collars that had been worn for a generation : that is to say, they had a modest round or V opening (No. 224), which shocked the clergy in all countries. All the German bishops combined in a pastoral letter attacking modern fashions. This is less surprising — in view of the Germans' indifference to fashion until recent years — than the fact that in spring 1914 a committee of aristocratic Parisians protested against dresses revealing the legs (No. 220).[1] But these minor conflicts were forgotten at the outbreak of a far greater one.

Draperies and tunics were only extraneous additions to the vertical line, which since 1910 has triumphed over curves in the Battle of the Bulge. Apart from occasional periods of flared skirts — during the Great War, the 1930s, Dior's New Look and other short-lived attempts at revival since World War II — the straight vertical line remains the basic principle of modern dress. We take it so much for granted, that we are apt to forget that in the whole history of European feminine fashion simple, slim, undraped skirts were worn only during the first fifteen or twenty years of the nineteenth century and on a small proportion of 'Empire' dresses in the late 1860s. Though it seems improbable that tight-lacing, curves, and voluminous skirts will ever return, considering the completely changed conditions which govern women's lives and activities, for purely social occasions no form of dress can be ruled out provided one can shuffle into a car wearing it.

[1] Max von Boehn, *Die Mode: Menschen und Moden im neunzehnten Jahrhundert*, Vol. IV, 1878–1914, Munich n.d. (1919).

BIBLIOGRAPHY AND STUDY LIST

ALISON ADBURGHAM, 'A Punch History of Manners and Modes : 1841–1940', London, 1961.

MRS. ADA S. BALLIN, 'The Science of Dress in Theory and Practice', London, 1885.

MRS. ADA S. BALLIN, 'Health and Beauty in Dress' (third edition of above), London, 1893.

CECIL BEATON, 'The Glass of Fashion', London, 1954.

(SIR) MAX BEERBOHM, 'A Defence of Cosmetics'. Article in *The Yellow Book*, London, April 1894.

PEARL BINDER, 'The Peacock's Tail', London, 1958.

QUENTIN BELL, 'On Human Finery', London, 1947.

CHARLES BLANC, 'Art and Ornament in Dress', London, 1877.

MATTHEW BLAIR, 'The Paisley Shawl, and the Men Who Produced It', Paisley, 1904.

MAX VON BOEHN, 'Die Mode: Menschen und Moden im neunzehnten Jahrhundert', fourth edition, Munich, n.d. (1919, 1920).

MAX VON BOEHN, 'Modes and Manners of the Nineteenth Century' (English translation of above), London, 1927.

MAX VON BOEHN, 'Das Beiwerk der Mode. Spitzen, Fächer, Handschuhe, Stöcke, Schirme, Schmuck', Munich, 1928.

MAX VON BOEHN, 'Vom Kaiserreich zur Republik', Berlin, 1917.

HENRI BOUCHOT, 'Les Elégances du Second Empire', Paris, n.d. (1897).

IRIS BROOKE, 'English Children's Costume since 1775' with an introduction by James Laver, London, 1930.

IRIS BROOKE, 'English Costume 1900–1950', London, 1951.

ANNE BUCK, 'Victorian Costume and Costume Accessories', London, 1961.

VISCOUNT BURY AND G. LACY HILLIER, 'Cycling', London, 1887.

DION CLAYTON CALTHROP, 'Winterhalter and the Crinoline'. Article in *The Connoisseur*, London, 1911.

DION CLAYTON CALTHROP, 'English Dress from Victoria to George V', London, 1934.

AUGUSTIN CHALLAMEL, 'The History of Fashion in France', London, 1882.

C. Compaign and L. Devere, 'The Tailor's Guide', 2 vols., London, 1855, 1856.

Cecil Willett Cunnington, 'The Perfect Lady', London, 1928.

C. W. Cunnington, 'Feminine Attitudes in the Nineteenth Century', London, 1935.

C. W. Cunnington, 'English Women's Clothing in the Nineteenth Century', London, 1937.

C. W. Cunnington, 'Why Women Wear Clothes', London, 1941.

C. W. Cunnington, 'The Art of English Costume', London, 1948.

C. W. Cunnington, 'Women', London, 1950.

C. W. Cunnington, 'English Women's Clothing in the Present Century', London, 1952.

C. W. and Phillis Cunnington, 'The History of Underclothes', London, 1951.

C. W. and P. Cunnington, 'Handbook of English Costume in the Nineteenth Century', London, 1959.

Millia Davenport, 'The Book of Costume', New York, 1948.

Sir William Henry Flower, 'Fashion in Deformity', London, 1881.

J. C. Fluegel, 'The Psychology of Clothes', London, 1930.

Madge Garland, 'The Changing Face of Beauty', London, 1957.

Florence Mary Gardner, 'The Evolution of Fashion', London, 1897.

Charles Gibbs-Smith, 'The Fashionable Lady in the Nineteenth Century', London, 1960.

Carrie A. Hall, 'From Hoopskirts to Nudity. A Review of the Follies and Foibles of Fashion 1866–1936', Caldwell, Idaho, 1938.

Henny Harald Hansen, 'Knaurs Kostümbuch', Munich and Zürich, 1956.

Viscountess Harberton, 'Reasons for Reform in Dress', London, n.d. (c. 1885).

Alfred C. Harmsworth and others, 'Motors and Motor-Driving', second edition, London, 1902.

Mrs. Mary Eliza Haweis, 'The Art of Beauty', London, 1878.

Mrs. Mary Eliza Haweis, 'The Art of Dress', London, 1879.

Henry FitzGerald Heard, 'Narcissus, an Anatomy of Clothes', London, 1925.

H. & M. Hiler, 'A Bibliography of Costume' (8000 titles), New York, 1939.

Angus Holden, 'Elegant Modes in the Nineteenth Century', London, 1935.

Carl Köhler, 'History of Costume', London, Bombay and Sydney, 1928. *

Anny Latour, 'Kings of Fashion', London, 1958.

James Laver, 'Fashions and Fashion Plates 1800–1900', London, 1943.

*Dover reprint.

JAMES LAVER, 'Taste and Fashion from the French Revolution to the Present Day', new and revised edition, London, 1945.

JAMES LAVER, 'Costume Illustration. The Nineteenth Century', London, 1947.

JAMES LAVER, 'Dress', London, 1950.

JAMES LAVER, 'Children's Fashions in the Nineteenth Century', London, 1951.

JAMES LAVER, 'Clothes', London, 1952.

JAMES LAVER and IRIS BROOKE, 'English Costume of the Nineteenth Century', London, 1929.

DOROTHY LEVITT, 'The Woman and the Car', London, 1909.

'LUKE LIMNER' (JOHN LEIGHTON), 'Madre Natura versus the Moloch of Fashion: a Social Essay', London, 1870, fourth edition 1874.

MRS. ELIZA LYNN LINTON, 'The Girl of the Period', London, 1868. (Articles reprinted from *The Saturday Review*.)

MRS. MARY PHILADELPHIA MERRIFIELD. 'Dress as a Fine Art'. London, 1854. (Reprinted from articles in *The Art Journal* and *Sharpe's London Magazine*.)

DORIS LANGLEY MOORE, 'The Woman in Fashion', London, 1949.

DORIS LANGLEY MOORE, 'The Child in Fashion', London, 1953.

ELIAS MOSES & SON, 'Fashions for 1857', London, n.d. (1856). Contains earlier pamphlets bound in.

ELIAS MOSES & SON, 'Gossip on Dress', London, 1863.

ELIAS MOSES & SON, 'On Modern Costume', London, 1863.

ELIAS MOSES & SON, 'The Philosophy of Dress', London, 1864.

HANS MÜTZEL, 'Vom Lendenschurz zur Modetracht', Berlin, 1925.

HERBERT NORRIS and OSWALD CURTIS, 'Costume and Fashion', Vol. VI, Nineteenth Century, London, 1933.

MRS. MARGARET OLIPHANT, 'Dress', London, 1878.

WALBURGA, LADY PAGET, 'Scenes and Memories', London, 1912.

MRS. C. S. PEEL, 'A Hundred Wonderful Years', London, 1926.

EDWARD PHILPOTT, 'Crinoline in our Parks and Promenades from 1710 to 1864', London, n.d. (1864).

DAVID PIPER, 'The English Face', London, 1957.

CAMILLE PITON, 'Le Costume Civil en France du XIIIe au XIXe Siècle', Paris, n.d. (1913).

PAUL POIRET, 'En Habillant l'Epoque', Paris, 1930.

JULIUS M. PRICE, 'Dame Fashion: Paris–London (1786–1912)', London, 1913.

Bibliography and Study List

MRS. ERIC PRITCHARD, 'The Cult of Chiffon', London, 1902.

MARJORIE AND C. H. B. QUENNELL, 'A History of Everyday Things in England', fifth edition, London, 1952–3.

PETER QUENNELL, 'Victorian Panorama', London, 1937.

WOLFGANG QUINCKE, 'Handbuch der Kostümkunde'. 1896.

REGINALD REYNOLDS, 'Beards. An omnium gatherum', London, 1950.

JACQUES RUPPERT, 'Le Costume', Paris, 1931.

ALISON SETTLE, 'English Fashion', London, 1948.

EDITH SAUNDERS, 'The Age of Worth', London, 1954.

SACHEVERELL SITWELL, 'La Vie Parisienne: a Tribute to Offenbach', London, 1937.

HIPPOLYTE TAINE, 'Notes on England', translated by Edward Hyams, London, 1957.

(SIR) FREDERICK TREVES, 'Influence of Clothing on Health', London, n.d. (1886).

(SIR) FREDERICK TREVES, 'The Dress of the Period in its Relations to Health', London, n.d. (1887).

NEVIL TRUMAN, 'Historic Costume', London, 1936.

OCTAVE UZANNE, 'The Sunshade, the Glove, the Muff', London, 1883.

OCTAVE UZANNE, 'Fashion in Paris', London, 1898.

OCTAVE UZANNE, 'L'Art et les Artifices de Beauté', Paris, n.d. (c. 1903).

E. WARD & Co., 'Dress Reform Problem', London and Bradford, 1886.

G. F. WATTS, 'On Taste in Dress'. Article in *The Nineteenth Century*, Jan. 1883.

NORAH WAUGH, 'Corsets and Crinolines', London, 1954.

WILLIAM MARK WEBB, 'The Heritage of Dress', London, 1907.

RUTH TURNER WILCOX, 'The Mode in Hats and Headdress', New York, 1945.

RUTH TURNER WILCOX. 'The Mode in Costume', New York, 1946.

OSCAR WILDE, 'Art and Decoration', London, 1920. (Posthumously published lectures and articles.)

OSCAR WILDE, 'Essays and Lectures by Oscar Wilde', sixth edition, London, 1928.

JACQUES WILHELM, 'La Vie à Paris sous le Second Empire et la Troisième République', Paris, 1947.

JEAN PHILIPPE WORTH, 'A Century of Fashion', Boston, 1928.

DR. ANDREW WYNTER, 'Peeps into the Human Hive', London, 1874.

ANONYMOUS, 'Beard-shaving, and the common use of the Razor' (by William Henry Henshawe), London, 1847.

'Music; and the Art of Dress'. London, 1852. (Reprinted from *The Quarterly Review*, March 1847.)

'Crinoline und Amazonenhut, oder Anecdoten fuer Freunde und Feinde der Crinoline und des "letzten Versuchs"', second edition, Nordhausen, 1858.

'Crinoline', London, n.d. (1863). (Reprinted from *The Illustrated News of the World.*)

'The Corset and the Crinoline' (by W.B.L.), London, n.d. (1868).

CATALOGUES

'The Literature of Fashion', National Book League catalogue, by James Laver, London, 1947.

London Museum Catalogues, No. 5 'Costume', by Thalassa Cruso, London, 1946.

Victoria and Albert Museum, 'Costume Illustration. The Nineteenth Century', Introduction by James Laver, London, 1947.

Victoria and Albert Museum, 'A Brief Guide to the Costume Court' by Madeleine Blumstein, London, 1962.

PERIODICALS

CIBA Review No. 38, 1941. Also No. 46, 1943.

The Court Magazine and Monthly Critic and Ladies' Magazine and Museum of the Belles Lettres, Music, Fine Arts, Drama, Fashion, etc.

The Englishwoman's Domestic Magazine.

Fashions of Today.

Le Follet.

The Gazette of Fashion.

The Illustrated London News.

Le Journal des Costumes.

Le Journal des Demoiselles.

The Ladies' Cabinet.

* *The Ladies' Cabinet of Fashion, Music and Romance.*

* *The Ladies' Companion.*

The Ladies' Gazette of Fashion.

The Lady.

The Lady Cyclist.

The Lady's Newspaper.

The Lady's Pictorial.

The Lady's Realm.

The Lady's Treasury.

The Lady's World (continued as *The Woman's World*).

The Milliner and Dressmaker.

Les Modes.

Les Modes Parisiennes et Journal du Beaumonde.

Myra's Journal of Dress and Fashion.

* *The New Monthly Belle Assemblée.*

The Portfolio of Ladies' Fashions.

* N.B. *The Ladies' Cabinet* from July 1852 is identical with *The New Monthly Belle Assemblée*, and *Ladies' Companion*.

Punch.

The Queen.

The Rational Dress Society's Gazette.

The Sphere.

The Tailor and Cutter.

The World of Fashion.

The Young Englishwoman.

The Young Lady's Journal.

INDEX

Index

Index

A CATALOG OF SELECTED
DOVER BOOKS
IN ALL FIELDS OF INTEREST

A CATALOG OF SELECTED DOVER
BOOKS IN ALL FIELDS OF INTEREST

CONCERNING THE SPIRITUAL IN ART, Wassily Kandinsky. Pioneering work by father of abstract art. Thoughts on color theory, nature of art. Analysis of earlier masters. 12 illustrations. 80pp. of text. 5⅜ x 8½.　　　　　　0-486-23411-8

CELTIC ART: The Methods of Construction, George Bain. Simple geometric techniques for making Celtic interlacements, spirals, Kells-type initials, animals, humans, etc. Over 500 illustrations. 160pp. 9 x 12. (Available in U.S. only.)　　　0-486-22923-8

AN ATLAS OF ANATOMY FOR ARTISTS, Fritz Schider. Most thorough reference work on art anatomy in the world. Hundreds of illustrations, including selections from works by Vesalius, Leonardo, Goya, Ingres, Michelangelo, others. 593 illustrations. 192pp. 7⅛ x 10¼.　　　　　　　　　　　　0-486-20241-0

CELTIC HAND STROKE-BY-STROKE (Irish Half-Uncial from "The Book of Kells"): An Arthur Baker Calligraphy Manual, Arthur Baker. Complete guide to creating each letter of the alphabet in distinctive Celtic manner. Covers hand position, strokes, pens, inks, paper, more. Illustrated. 48pp. 8¼ x 11.　0-486-24336-2

EASY ORIGAMI, John Montroll. Charming collection of 32 projects (hat, cup, pelican, piano, swan, many more) specially designed for the novice origami hobbyist. Clearly illustrated easy-to-follow instructions insure that even beginning papercrafters will achieve successful results. 48pp. 8¼ x 11.　　　　0-486-27298-2

BLOOMINGDALE'S ILLUSTRATED 1886 CATALOG: Fashions, Dry Goods and Housewares, Bloomingdale Brothers. Famed merchants' extremely rare catalog depicting about 1,700 products: clothing, housewares, firearms, dry goods, jewelry, more. Invaluable for dating, identifying vintage items. Also, copyright-free graphics for artists, designers. Co-published with Henry Ford Museum & Greenfield Village. 160pp. 8¼ x 11.　　　　　　　　　　　　　　　　0-486-25780-0

THE ART OF WORLDLY WISDOM, Baltasar Gracian. "Think with the few and speak with the many," "Friends are a second existence," and "Be able to forget" are among this 1637 volume's 300 pithy maxims. A perfect source of mental and spiritual refreshment, it can be opened at random and appreciated either in brief or at length. 128pp. 5⅜ x 8½.　　　　　　　　　　　　　　　0-486-44034-6

JOHNSON'S DICTIONARY: A Modern Selection, Samuel Johnson (E. L. McAdam and George Milne, eds.). This modern version reduces the original 1755 edition's 2,300 pages of definitions and literary examples to a more manageable length, retaining the verbal pleasure and historical curiosity of the original. 480pp. 5³⁄₁₆ x 8¼.　　　　　　　　　　　　　　　　　0-486-44089-3

ADVENTURES OF HUCKLEBERRY FINN, Mark Twain, Illustrated by E. W. Kemble. A work of eternal richness and complexity, a source of ongoing critical debate, and a literary landmark, Twain's 1885 masterpiece about a barefoot boy's journey of self-discovery has enthralled readers around the world. This handsome clothbound reproduction of the first edition features all 174 of the original black-and-white illustrations. 368pp. 5⅜ x 8½.　　　　　　　　　0-486-44322-1

STICKLEY CRAFTSMAN FURNITURE CATALOGS, Gustav Stickley and L. & J. G. Stickley. Beautiful, functional furniture in two authentic catalogs from 1910. 594 illustrations, including 277 photos, show settles, rockers, armchairs, reclining chairs, bookcases, desks, tables. 183pp. 6½ x 9¼. 0-486-23838-5

AMERICAN LOCOMOTIVES IN HISTORIC PHOTOGRAPHS: 1858 to 1949, Ron Ziel (ed.). A rare collection of 126 meticulously detailed official photographs, called "builder portraits," of American locomotives that majestically chronicle the rise of steam locomotive power in America. Introduction. Detailed captions. xi+ 129pp. 9 x 12. 0-486-27393-8

AMERICA'S LIGHTHOUSES: An Illustrated History, Francis Ross Holland, Jr. Delightfully written, profusely illustrated fact-filled survey of over 200 American lighthouses since 1716. History, anecdotes, technological advances, more. 240pp. 8 x 10¾. 0-486-25576-X

TOWARDS A NEW ARCHITECTURE, Le Corbusier. Pioneering manifesto by founder of "International School." Technical and aesthetic theories, views of industry, economics, relation of form to function, "mass-production split" and much more. Profusely illustrated. 320pp. 6⅛ x 9¼. (Available in U.S. only.) 0-486-25023 7

HOW THE OTHER HALF LIVES, Jacob Riis. Famous journalistic record, exposing poverty and degradation of New York slums around 1900, by major social reformer. 100 striking and influential photographs. 233pp. 10 x 7⅞. 0-486-22012-5

FRUIT KEY AND TWIG KEY TO TREES AND SHRUBS, William M. Harlow. One of the handiest and most widely used identification aids. Fruit key covers 120 deciduous and evergreen species; twig key 160 deciduous species. Easily used. Over 300 photographs. 126pp. 5⅜ x 8½. 0-486-20511-8

COMMON BIRD SONGS, Dr. Donald J. Borror. Songs of 60 most common U.S. birds: robins, sparrows, cardinals, bluejays, finches, more—arranged in order of increasing complexity. Up to 9 variations of songs of each species.
Cassette and manual 0-486-99911-4

ORCHIDS AS HOUSE PLANTS, Rebecca Tyson Northen. Grow cattleyas and many other kinds of orchids—in a window, in a case, or under artificial light. 63 illustrations. 148pp. 5⅜ x 8½. 0-486-23261-1

MONSTER MAZES, Dave Phillips. Masterful mazes at four levels of difficulty. Avoid deadly perils and evil creatures to find magical treasures. Solutions for all 32 exciting illustrated puzzles. 48pp. 8¼ x 11. 0-486-26005-4

MOZART'S DON GIOVANNI (DOVER OPERA LIBRETTO SERIES), Wolfgang Amadeus Mozart. Introduced and translated by Ellen H. Bleiler. Standard Italian libretto, with complete English translation. Convenient and thoroughly portable—an ideal companion for reading along with a recording or the performance itself. Introduction. List of characters. Plot summary. 121pp. 5¼ x 8½. 0-486-24944-1

FRANK LLOYD WRIGHT'S DANA HOUSE, Donald Hoffmann. Pictorial essay of residential masterpiece with over 160 interior and exterior photos, plans, elevations, sketches and studies. 128pp. 9¼ x 10¾. 0-486-29120-0

THE CLARINET AND CLARINET PLAYING, David Pino. Lively, comprehensive work features suggestions about technique, musicianship, and musical interpretation, as well as guidelines for teaching, making your own reeds, and preparing for public performance. Includes an intriguing look at clarinet history. "A godsend," *The Clarinet,* Journal of the International Clarinet Society. Appendixes. 7 illus. 320pp. 5⅜ x 8½.   0-486-40270-3

HOLLYWOOD GLAMOR PORTRAITS, John Kobal (ed.). 145 photos from 1926-49. Harlow, Gable, Bogart, Bacall; 94 stars in all. Full background on photographers, technical aspects. 160pp. 8⅜ x 11¼.   0-486-23352-9

THE RAVEN AND OTHER FAVORITE POEMS, Edgar Allan Poe. Over 40 of the author's most memorable poems: "The Bells," "Ulalume," "Israfel," "To Helen," "The Conqueror Worm," "Eldorado," "Annabel Lee," many more. Alphabetic lists of titles and first lines. 64pp. 5³/₁₆ x 8¼.   0-486-26685-0

PERSONAL MEMOIRS OF U. S. GRANT, Ulysses Simpson Grant. Intelligent, deeply moving firsthand account of Civil War campaigns, considered by many the finest military memoirs ever written. Includes letters, historic photographs, maps and more. 528pp. 6⅛ x 9¼.   0-486-28587-1

POE ILLUSTRATED: Art by Doré, Dulac, Rackham and Others, selected and edited by Jeff A. Menges. More than 100 compelling illustrations, in brilliant color and crisp black-and-white, include scenes from "The Raven," "The Pit and the Pendulum," "The Gold-Bug," and other stories and poems. 96pp. 8⅜ x 11.
0-486-45746-X

RUSSIAN STORIES/RUSSKIE RASSKAZY: A Dual-Language Book, edited by Gleb Struve. Twelve tales by such masters as Chekhov, Tolstoy, Dostoevsky, Pushkin, others. Excellent word-for-word English translations on facing pages, plus teaching and study aids, Russian/English vocabulary, biographical/critical introductions, more. 416pp. 5⅜ x 8½.   0-486-26244-8

PHILADELPHIA THEN AND NOW: 60 Sites Photographed in the Past and Present, Kenneth Finkel and Susan Oyama. Rare photographs of City Hall, Logan Square, Independence Hall, Betsy Ross House, other landmarks juxtaposed with contemporary views. Captures changing face of historic city. Introduction. Captions. 128pp. 8¼ x 11.   0-486-25790-8

NORTH AMERICAN INDIAN LIFE: Customs and Traditions of 23 Tribes, Elsie Clews Parsons (ed.). 27 fictionalized essays by noted anthropologists examine religion, customs, government, additional facets of life among the Winnebago, Crow, Zuni, Eskimo, other tribes. 480pp. 6⅛ x 9¼.   0-486-27377-6

TECHNICAL MANUAL AND DICTIONARY OF CLASSICAL BALLET, Gail Grant. Defines, explains, comments on steps, movements, poses and concepts. 15-page pictorial section. Basic book for student, viewer. 127pp. 5⅜ x 8½.
0-486-21843-0

THE MALE AND FEMALE FIGURE IN MOTION: 60 Classic Photographic Sequences, Eadweard Muybridge. 60 true-action photographs of men and women walking, running, climbing, bending, turning, etc., reproduced from a rare 19th-century masterpiece. vi + 121pp. 9 x 12.   0-486-24745-7

ANIMALS: 1,419 Copyright-Free Illustrations of Mammals, Birds, Fish, Insects, etc., Jim Harter (ed.). Clear wood engravings present, in extremely lifelike poses, over 1,000 species of animals. One of the most extensive pictorial sourcebooks of its kind. Captions. Index. 284pp. 9 x 12. 0-486-23766-4

1001 QUESTIONS ANSWERED ABOUT THE SEASHORE, N. J. Berrill and Jacquelyn Berrill. Queries answered about dolphins, sea snails, sponges, starfish, fishes, shore birds, many others. Covers appearance, breeding, growth, feeding, much more. 305pp. 5¼ x 8¼. 0-486-23366-9

ATTRACTING BIRDS TO YOUR YARD, William J. Weber. Easy-to-follow guide offers advice on how to attract the greatest diversity of birds: birdhouses, feeders, water and waterers, much more. 96pp. 5³⁄₁₆ x 8¼. 0-486-28927-3

MEDICINAL AND OTHER USES OF NORTH AMERICAN PLANTS: A Historical Survey with Special Reference to the Eastern Indian Tribes, Charlotte Erichsen-Brown. Chronological historical citations document 500 years of usage of plants, trees, shrubs native to eastern Canada, northeastern U.S. Also complete identifying information. 343 illustrations. 544pp. 6½ x 9¼. 0-486-25951-X

STORYBOOK MAZES, Dave Phillips. 23 stories and mazes on two-page spreads: Wizard of Oz, Treasure Island, Robin Hood, etc. Solutions. 64pp. 8¼ x 11.
0-486-23628-5

AMERICAN NEGRO SONGS: 230 Folk Songs and Spirituals, Religious and Secular, John W. Work. This authoritative study traces the African influences of songs sung and played by black Americans at work, in church, and as entertainment. The author discusses the lyric significance of such songs as "Swing Low, Sweet Chariot," "John Henry," and others and offers the words and music for 230 songs. Bibliography. Index of Song Titles. 272pp. 6½ x 9¼. 0-486-40271-1

MOVIE-STAR PORTRAITS OF THE FORTIES, John Kobal (ed.). 163 glamor, studio photos of 106 stars of the 1940s: Rita Hayworth, Ava Gardner, Marlon Brando, Clark Gable, many more. 176pp. 8⅜ x 11¼. 0-486-23546-7

YEKL and THE IMPORTED BRIDEGROOM AND OTHER STORIES OF YIDDISH NEW YORK, Abraham Cahan. Film Hester Street based on Yekl (1896). Novel, other stories among first about Jewish immigrants on N.Y.'s East Side. 240pp. 5⅜ x 8½. 0-486-22427-9

SELECTED POEMS, Walt Whitman. Generous sampling from Leaves of Grass. Twenty-four poems include "I Hear America Singing," "Song of the Open Road," "I Sing the Body Electric," "When Lilacs Last in the Dooryard Bloom'd," "O Captain! My Captain!"—all reprinted from an authoritative edition. Lists of titles and first lines. 128pp. 5³⁄₁₆ x 8¼. 0-486-26878-0

SONGS OF EXPERIENCE: Facsimile Reproduction with 26 Plates in Full Color, William Blake. 26 full-color plates from a rare 1826 edition. Includes "The Tyger," "London," "Holy Thursday," and other poems. Printed text of poems. 48pp. 5¼ x 7.
0-486-24636-1

THE BEST TALES OF HOFFMANN, E. T. A. Hoffmann. 10 of Hoffmann's most important stories: "Nutcracker and the King of Mice," "The Golden Flowerpot," etc. 458pp. 5⅜ x 8½. 0-486-21793-0

THE BOOK OF TEA, Kakuzo Okakura. Minor classic of the Orient: entertaining, charming explanation, interpretation of traditional Japanese culture in terms of tea ceremony. 94pp. 5⅜ x 8½. 0-486-20070-1

MAKING FURNITURE MASTERPIECES: 30 Projects with Measured Drawings, Franklin H. Gottshall. Step-by-step instructions, illustrations for constructing handsome, useful pieces, among them a Sheraton desk, Chippendale chair, Spanish desk, Queen Anne table and a William and Mary dressing mirror. 224pp. 8⅛ x 11¼.
0-486-29338-6

NORTH AMERICAN INDIAN DESIGNS FOR ARTISTS AND CRAFTSPEOPLE, Eva Wilson. Over 360 authentic copyright-free designs adapted from Navajo blankets, Hopi pottery, Sioux buffalo hides, more. Geometrics, symbolic figures, plant and animal motifs, etc. 128pp. 8⅜ x 11. (Not for sale in the United Kingdom.) 0-486-25341-4

THE FOSSIL BOOK: A Record of Prehistoric Life, Patricia V. Rich et al. Profusely illustrated definitive guide covers everything from single-celled organisms and dinosaurs to birds and mammals and the interplay between climate and man. Over 1,500 illustrations. 760pp. 7½ x 10⅛. 0-486-29371-8

VICTORIAN ARCHITECTURAL DETAILS: Designs for Over 700 Stairs, Mantels, Doors, Windows, Cornices, Porches, and Other Decorative Elements, A. J. Bicknell & Company. Everything from dormer windows and piazzas to balconies and gable ornaments. Also includes elevations and floor plans for handsome, private residences and commercial structures. 80pp. 9⅜ x 12¼. 0-486-44015-X

WESTERN ISLAMIC ARCHITECTURE: A Concise Introduction, John D. Hoag. Profusely illustrated critical appraisal compares and contrasts Islamic mosques and palaces–from Spain and Egypt to other areas in the Middle East. 139 illustrations. 128pp. 6 x 9. 0-486-43760-4

CHINESE ARCHITECTURE: A Pictorial History, Liang Ssu-ch'eng. More than 240 rare photographs and drawings depict temples, pagodas, tombs, bridges, and imperial palaces comprising much of China's architectural heritage. 152 halftones, 94 diagrams. 232pp. 10¾ x 9⅞. 0-486-43999-2

THE RENAISSANCE: Studies in Art and Poetry, Walter Pater. One of the most talked-about books of the 19th century, *The Renaissance* combines scholarship and philosophy in an innovative work of cultural criticism that examines the achievements of Botticelli, Leonardo, Michelangelo, and other artists. "The holy writ of beauty."–Oscar Wilde. 160pp. 5⅜ x 8½. 0-486-44025-7

A TREATISE ON PAINTING, Leonardo da Vinci. The great Renaissance artist's practical advice on drawing and painting techniques covers anatomy, perspective, composition, light and shadow, and color. A classic of art instruction, it features 48 drawings by Nicholas Poussin and Leon Battista Alberti. 192pp. 5⅜ x 8½.
0-486-44155-5

THE ESSENTIAL JEFFERSON, Thomas Jefferson, edited by John Dewey. This extraordinary primer offers a superb survey of Jeffersonian thought. It features writings on political and economic philosophy, morals and religion, intellectual freedom and progress, education, secession, slavery, and more. 176pp. 5⅜ x 8½.
0-486-46599-3

WASHINGTON IRVING'S RIP VAN WINKLE, Illustrated by Arthur Rackham. Lovely prints that established artist as a leading illustrator of the time and forever etched into the popular imagination a classic of Catskill lore. 51 full-color plates. 80pp. 8⅜ x 11. 0-486-44242-X

HENSCHE ON PAINTING, John W. Robichaux. Basic painting philosophy and methodology of a great teacher, as expounded in his famous classes and workshops on Cape Cod. 7 illustrations in color on covers. 80pp. 5⅜ x 8½. 0-486-43728-0

CATALOG OF DOVER BOOKS

LIGHT AND SHADE: A Classic Approach to Three-Dimensional Drawing, Mrs. Mary P. Merrifield. Handy reference clearly demonstrates principles of light and shade by revealing effects of common daylight, sunshine, and candle or artificial light on geometrical solids. 13 plates. 64pp. 5⅜ x 8½. 0-486-44143-1

ASTROLOGY AND ASTRONOMY: A Pictorial Archive of Signs and Symbols, Ernst and Johanna Lehner. Treasure trove of stories, lore, and myth, accompanied by more than 300 rare illustrations of planets, the Milky Way, signs of the zodiac, comets, meteors, and other astronomical phenomena. 102pp. 8⅜ x 11. 0-486-43981-X

JEWELRY MAKING: Techniques for Metal, Tim McCreight. Easy-to-follow instructions and carefully executed illustrations describe tools and techniques, use of gems and enamels, wire inlay, casting, and other topics. 72 line illustrations and diagrams. 176pp. 8¼ x 10⅞. 0-486-44043-5

MAKING BIRDHOUSES: Easy and Advanced Projects, Gladstone Califf. Easy-to-follow instructions include diagrams for everything from a one-room house for bluebirds to a forty-two-room structure for purple martins. 56 plates; 4 figures. 80pp. 8¾ x 6⅜. 0-486-44183-0

LITTLE BOOK OF LOG CABINS: How to Build and Furnish Them, William S. Wicks. Handy how-to manual, with instructions and illustrations for building cabins in the Adirondack style, fireplaces, stairways, furniture, beamed ceilings, and more. 102 line drawings. 96pp. 8¾ x 6⅜. 0-486-44259-4

THE SEASONS OF AMERICA PAST, Eric Sloane. From "sugaring time" and strawberry picking to Indian summer and fall harvest, a whole year's activities described in charming prose and enhanced with 79 of the author's own illustrations. 160pp. 8¼ x 11. 0-486-44220-9

THE METROPOLIS OF TOMORROW, Hugh Ferriss. Generous, prophetic vision of the metropolis of the future, as perceived in 1929. Powerful illustrations of towering structures, wide avenues, and rooftop parks–all features in many of today's modern cities. 59 illustrations. 144pp. 8¼ x 11. 0-486-43727-2

THE PATH TO ROME, Hilaire Belloc. This 1902 memoir abounds in lively vignettes from a vanished time, recounting a pilgrimage on foot across the Alps and Apennines in order to "see all Europe which the Christian Faith has saved." 77 of the author's original line drawings complement his sparkling prose. 272pp. 5⅜ x 8½. 0-486-44001-X

THE HISTORY OF RASSELAS: Prince of Abissinia, Samuel Johnson. Distinguished English writer attacks eighteenth-century optimism and man's unrealistic estimates of what life has to offer. 112pp. 5⅜ x 8½. 0-486-44094-X

A VOYAGE TO ARCTURUS, David Lindsay. A brilliant flight of pure fancy, where wild creatures crowd the fantastic landscape and demented torturers dominate victims with their bizarre mental powers. 272pp. 5⅜ x 8½. 0-486-44198-9

Paperbound unless otherwise indicated. Available at your book dealer, online at **www.doverpublications.com**, or by writing to Dept. GI, Dover Publications, Inc., 31 East 2nd Street, Mineola, NY 11501. For current price information or for free catalogs (please indicate field of interest), write to Dover Publications or log on to **www.doverpublications.com** and see every Dover book in print. Dover publishes more than 400 books each year on science, elementary and advanced mathematics, biology, music, art, literary history, social sciences, and other areas.